"*Letter to Theo* surveys the biblical passages relating to the role of women in the church. It not only answers many questions raised by Evangelicals but it ensures women an equal role in exercising spiritual gifts and receiving a divine call to ministry."

—Charles A. Estridge
Vice President for Academic Affairs
Central Bible College

"Women, called of God to preach the Gospel, labored throughout the New Testament church from its inception. Elbert's detailed defense of such able ministry in "Pastoral Letter to Theo" is a great read indeed. Some have opposed the role of women in ministry, but Elbert carefully and accurately delineates the biblical record in support of God-called female preachers. Wow! What a heritage of leadership and of preachers, ministers and missionaries can be found in the Pentecostal movement, a portion of which is well-glimpsed in the Foreword to *Letter to Theo*. We should be proud of our position of ordaining and supporting women in ministry."

—Talmadge L. French
Provost
Apostolic School of Theology

"Paul Elbert frames his pastoral exhortations as a letter to a ministerial candidate, Theo. In this "user friendly" way he presents an analysis by which Theo would not merely propagate the long-held doctrinal traditions of some by simple proof-texting. He uses what is for some a "hot topic," women in ministry, to illustrate what happens when this proof-texting method is uncritically applied. In marked contrast, he shows the results of a more thorough historical, socio-cultural interpretation which more appropriately and accurately addresses the situations of the text. Of course we all realize, although the culture of our world is not the same as in Paul's day, that there are timeless, changeless truths which apply cross-culturally and over time. Elbert dynamically demonstrates the dangers of interpreting a text uncritically via unarticulated preconceptions. This is certainly something all preachers, teachers, and pastors need to consider as they approach the rigors and challenges of ministering in the world of the twentieth-first century. As the daughter of Dr. Bebe Patton, Founder, Pastor and Teacher, Patten University & Christian Cathedral, a woman evangelist/pastor who ministered for over 75 years, I also applaud how professor Elbert addresses the issue of women in ministry and pray that his words have the needed impact to enable more of God's servants to effectively work in the vineyard of God."

—Rebecca Skaggs
Professor of New Testament and Greek
Patten University

"Although women who minister have contributed significantly within Pentecostalism, classical Pentecostal churches in some Western countries have generally become less welcoming. The kind of work done by Paul Elbert personalizing this issue serves as more than just an apologetic; it celebrates the important contributions of women who minister."

—David S. Norris
Professor of Biblical Theology
Urshan Graduate School of Theology

"Paul Elbert's *Letter to Theo* is both timely and practical. In it he expounds on the truth that Scripture, when it is extracted selectively and removed from its fuller context, can become endlessly malleable via an extreme form of theological interpretation. It can then be reduced to little more than a reflection of the reader's prejudices, cultural values, and needs. Elbert, on the other hand, argues persuasively that a contextually attuned reading of the New Testament, duly mindful of the real people involved in this Christian communication, results in the realization of women being actively invited to participate most fully in every aspect of Christian ministry. This realization is especially needed today in world evangelism."

—Scott Ellington
Adjunct Professor of Old Testament
Regent University

"Restricting women from leadership and ministry in the church is, as Paul Elbert deftly argues, based in faulty exegesis and naive proof-texting. The more serious, underlying issue is that proof-texting combined with dispensational cessationism is ultimately a form of eisegesis, a way of making Scripture say what you want it to say. A more faithful hermeneutic listens to the whole counsel of Scripture and interprets the Bible in its context, but with sensitivity to the contemporary world. *Pastoral Letter to Theo* is practical and encouraging advice for all ministers and is rooted in a contextually sensitive reading of the New Testament."

—Peter Althouse
Instructor in Theology
Tyndale University College and Seminary

"This well-researched presentation is a focused study resource for countering the dispensational/cessationist proof-texting culture of evangelical Protestantism, a tradition that has largely hamstrung women's ministry. *Letter to Theo* suggests that a re-evaluation of that position should be seriously considered. *Letter to Theo* is an exemplary case study in contextual interpretive method and will be of practical value particularly for grounding women's ministry in the local church according to what Luke, Paul, and other apostles believed."

—Tony G. Moon
Professor of Christian Ministries
Emmanuel College

"Paul Elbert's *Pastoral Letter to Theo* is a creative critique of the all too common misguided form of interpretation known as proof-texting. Alternatively, Elbert exhibits a historically sensitive interpretation guided primarily by literary context and overall narrative flow. *Letter to Theo* offers a concise, well-informed comment on the basics of sensible interpretation and a cohesive New Testament understanding of Christian women in ministry."

—Robby Waddell
Associate Professor of New Testament
Southeastern University

Pastoral Letter to Theo

Pastoral Letter to Theo

*An Introduction to Interpretation
and Women's Ministries*

Paul Elbert

WIPF & STOCK · Eugene, Oregon

PASTORAL LETTER TO THEO
An Introduction to Interpretation and Women's Ministries

ISBN 13: 978-1-55635-546-2

Manufactured in the U.S.A.

Other books by Paul Elbert published by Wipf & Stock:

Essays on Apostolic Themes: Studies in Honor of Howard M. Ervin
Faces of Renewal: Studies in Honor of Stanley M. Horton

Contents

Acknowledgment

I WOULD like to thank the faculty, staff, and administration of the Church of God Theological Seminary, Cleveland, Tennessee, for providing a cordial atmosphere in which the thoughts expressed here could develop. In particular, several women students from foreign lands in my Theological German classes started me thinking about these issues in a serious way. As they prepared for ministry on their native soils I knew that they probably would not be subjected to the questionable claims and Spirit-quenching intimidations to which Pentecostal/Charismatic women ministers are frequently subjected elsewhere. A faulty style of biblical interpretation is responsible for this circumstance, whereby women's ministries are either textually marginalized or asserted to have ceased under the ideological imprint of chasmal presuppositions. My work on Greco-Roman education and associated narrative-rhetorical methods of composition suggested to me that the interpretive or ideological style responsible for generating these questionable claims to which pastors, missionaries, students, laypersons, and scholars are exposed was far removed from the literary atmosphere of the New Testament world. Discussion with my colleagues, Kimberly Alexander and Cheryl Bridges Johns, also impressed me with the need to be more intentional about this particular dynamic of faith formation. The Holy Spirit is a powerful force and the heavenly Jesus is calling disciple-believers into the ministry in a gender-neutral manner. Nevertheless, persistent and dogmatic voices that deny this spiritual reality need to be answered by noticing what New Testament writers actually say. Global Pentecostalism and the international Charismatic Renewal are not rooted in the sixteenth-century philosophical debate about the miraculous or in the sometimes rationalistic piety and religious cultural norms of western Evangelicalism. This revival had an entirely different origin, the Azusa Street Centennial Anniversary having been celebrated with a world commemoration in Los Angeles in 2006. It brings the holistic message of the Five-Fold Gospel (a gospel identifying Jesus as savior, sanctifier, baptizer in the Holy Spirit, healer, and soon coming king) and a different hermeneutical method. Evangelizing the world according to the intentions of the earthly and heavenly Jesus requires the full workforce that was and is intended. I am grateful for the students of the seminary whose zeal and desire to labor for Christ both here and abroad have opened my eyes anew to this great need of our time. Accordingly, I would like to dedicate this little book to these compatriots in ministry who are faithfully responding to their vocational callings from Jesus, as well as to the memory of four distinguished women pioneers who have gone ahead, as described in the Foreword.

Abbreviations

AB	Anchor Bible
ATJ	*Ashland Theological Journal*
BETL	Bibliotheca Ephemeridum theologicarum Lovaniensium
BJS	Brown Judaic Studies
CBQ	*Catholic Biblical Quarterly*
Chm	*Churchman*
EDNT	*Exegetical Dictionary of the New Testament*
EQ	*Evangelical Quarterly*
FKDG	Forschungen zur Kirchen und Dogmengeschichte
FThSt	Frankfurter Theologische Studien
FRLANT	Forschungen zur Religion und Literatur des Alten und Neuen Testaments
IBS	*Irish Biblical Studies*
IJST	*International Journal of Systematic Theology*
ITQ	*Irish Theological Quarterly*
JETS	*Journal of the Evangelical Theological Society*
JGRChJ	*Journal of Greco-Roman Christianity and Judaism*
JPT	*Journal of Pentecostal Theology*
JPTSup	Journal of Pentecostal Theology Supplements
KEK	Kritisch-exegetischer Kommentar über das Neue Testament
LD	Lectio divina
NJB	New Jerusalem Bible

NovT	*Novum Testamentum*
NovTSup	Novum Testamentum Supplements
NTOA	Novum Testamentum et Orbis Antiquus
NTS	*New Testament Studies*
QD	Quaestiones disputatae
RSV	Revised Standard Version, 2nd edition
RTR	*Reformed Theological Review*
SBLSymS	Society of Biblical Literature Symposium Series
SUNT	Studien zum Umwelt des Neuen Testements
TrinJ	*Trinity Journal*
WMANT	Wissenschaftliche Monographien zum Alten und Neuen Testament
WUNT	Wissenschaftliche Untersuchungen zum Neuen Testament
ZNW	*Zeitschrift für die neutestamentliche Wissenschaft*

Foreword

As we train and equip ministers for the twenty-first century we need a balance between spiritual fire and reflection. Personal reception of the gift of the Holy Spirit from the heavenly Jesus opens a door for disciple-believers to develop a deeper understanding of the interior working of the Spirit as we attempt to take the gospel of the Lord Jesus Christ to the "ends of the earth" and to "regions beyond" (Acts 1:8; 2 Cor 10:16). Of course, many gospel facts can be preached under the anointing with a sufficient, but not a thorough, attention to levels of context. Preaching can vary appropriately in contextual depth according to hearers and situations. Yet, as we all realize, seriously considered attention to original meaning and authorial intent improves and strengthens preaching and teaching, promoting a deeper and more sustained understanding.

Going to regions beyond is also best done with preaching and teaching from accurate translations of the Greek New Testament, in concert with a complete workforce of disciple-believers, so as to accomplish all the ministries that need to be done. Going to regions beyond is also best done by employing an interpretive method that respectfully accords the writers of scripture the competence to write in a cohesive and coherent manner and to be understood on that basis. Their attention to theme, plot, and personification is worthy of respect. These narrative elements do not deserve to be shredded either by proof-texting or by modern secular relativism with its fuzzy antiliterary theories that eviscerate the authorial intent and original meaning rightfully attributed to competent biblical authors. Berlin, for example, in her presidential address to the Society of Biblical Literature, "Search for a New Biblical Hermeneutics,"[1] and Archer and I, in our critiques of an "Evangelical Historical Critical Method,"[2] have attempted in our various ways to alleviate interpretive quagmires, recognize unexamined allegiance to destructive and hidden presuppositions, and eliminate proof-texting, all of which so often retard all of the afore-mentioned interpretive priorities.

We are currently engaged in a dialogue between a more traditional academic theology and the new Pentecostal/Charismatic theology where it is crucial to acknowledge the creative and interactive power of the Holy Spirit with Christian disciple-believers who would go to regions beyond. Accordingly, I have suggested that an "Evangelical Critical Historical Method," traditional among some, with its baggage of unexamined presuppositions, needs to be redesigned, recalibrated, and ultimately replaced by an approach with additional sensitivity to plot, theme, repetition and variation, characterization, and personification along the lines of a "Pentecostal/Charismatic Narrative-Critical and Narrative-Rhetorical Method."[3] This new method would be committed to serious investigation of *storytime* actuality and concurrent *spacetime* actuality or historicity where the narratives of the four Evangelists and Acts constitute an authoritative form of theological discourse. In this method that I envision, authorial intent and original meaning are very real and authentic concepts that would be rightly afforded to intelligent New Testament writers who are influenced by Greco-Roman rhetorical communication of the first century. This narratively and rhetorically attuned

1. Berlin, "Search."
2. Archer, "Critique;" Elbert, "Potential."
3. Elbert, "Potential."

method would also realize that biblical texts were intended to refer beyond themselves to the truths of God's activity in the world. I suspect that this approach would appeal to many literary-minded readers of biblical texts, including Jewish and Arabic readers, in search of improved interpretive techniques. As a new interpretive strategy is forged it may be wise to keep in mind, insofar as one sector of Christendom is vitally concerned, that "Pentecostals cannot return to the modernist cessationist worldview, nor can they be numbered among the Neo-Fundamentalist or Non-Charismatic Evangelical Reformed traditions (which are still very much modernistic cessationists and hostile towards Pentecostalism). This worldview is what the Pentecostal/Charismatic Christians have helped to undermine."[4]

I believe that Paul wrote for people whom he expected would understand him. He anticipated his language pertaining to various situations and experiences to be understood, and the vast majority of it undoubtedly was understood by his original readers. However, we can reasonably suggest that the later anonymous writer—whom I will call Luke—of Luke-Acts (a literary, two-volume work addressed to Theophilus [Luke 1:3; Acts 1:1]) probably attempted to clarify Paul's Spirit-language in order to promote fresh re-readings of Paul's earlier letters. It would be especially critical that language pertaining to activities of the Holy Spirit and to the heavenly Jesus be correctly applied to Christian experience. What better guide could be used than that already established in early Christianity? Luke does not find it consistent with his narrative purpose of characterizing the life of Paul to quote long excerpts involving Spirit-language from Paul's letters, although he undoubtedly was familiar with them. (He quotes from two other letters that are useful for his narrative purpose.) However, Luke's clarification

---

4. Archer, "Critique," 153 (parenthesis his).

of what could be experientially unclear to later readers of Paul with respect to the work of the Holy Spirit would be reasonably accomplished in Luke-Acts by the employment, according to contemporary Greco-Roman narrative convention, of rhetorically expected examples and precedents of personal Spirit-reception. In Luke-Acts the first addressee, Theophilus, will find good examples and precedents of this Christian experience beginning with Acts 2:4, personification wherein similar or identical Pauline language is narratively employed. Theophilus, most likely a disciple-believer, could then be expected to identify with and to imitate these reliable examples and precedents, with God's help, in his own Christian life.

Many students of Paul and of Luke today believe, with good reason, as I will attempt to suggest, that the Spirit-retarding claims, artificially devised epochs, and temporal chasms between original and later New Testament readers as a whole, which have been imposed by Protestant scholarship and formally incorporated within some Evangelical faith traditions since the mid-nineteenth century, are inappropriate and need to be considered for retirement. Accordingly, ministers—men or women—who would seek the full anointing of God in the revivalist, restorationist, multiracial movement of global Pentecostalism and the international Charismatic Renewal, in harmonious collaboration with all believers everywhere who accept their divine calling, would be best served by considering a contextually sensitive approach to biblical interpretation in all of their varied ministries. By a contextually sensitive interpretive approach I mean one that first seeks the most accurate translation from the biblical languages, one that desires to be considerate of the contemporary communicative conventions in play at the time the biblical authors wrote, and one that is duly attentive to the literary efforts of coherence and consistency achieved by intelligent authors.

It is to these ends that I have attempted to prepare this little book, without the scholarly clutter of too many footnotes. This project began several years ago as a result of conversations with a sincere Bible student whom I will call "Theo." Theo is a preacher who is struggling with the proof-texting assertions that have traditionally been aimed by some against important aspects of Spirit-filled ministry (Spirit-filled being a contemporary Christian term appropriated experientially from the text of Acts 2:4, where disciple-believers are described as filled with the Holy Spirit, Luke perhaps adopting this descriptive interior term from common Christian communicative practice at the time of his composition). These extracted noncontextual assertions may be especially prominent among those employing what might be identified as "Bible-belt" type approaches to biblical authors, if I might use an imperfectly defined geographical metaphor to characterize a questionable style of interpretation. In this approach there is a marked tendency to employ snippets of information excised out of their literary contexts for uncritical support of supposedly biblical "truths" that are then promoted as absolute. This is not to doubt the sincerity of such extractive approaches to biblical authors, but simply to question the veracity or the legitimacy of this style of interpretation. The southeastern to the southern Midwest of the United States forms a kind of belt across part of that country, wherein some assertions as to "what the Bible says," especially regarding activities of the Holy Spirit and women's ministries, contributed to the coinage of the term "Bible Belt" as a way of referring to this distinctive style of interpretation, which of course does not apply to everyone who lives there.

While it is commendable for citizens of any country to take an interest in using the Bible, extravagant assertions stemming from historically intervening cultural and secular traditions rather than from biblical authors may reflect an excessive rational exuberance that is in need of correction or adjustment. Of course these kinds of ingrained ecclesiastical assertions are certainly not totally dormant in "Bible-belt" zones elsewhere, if I might appropriate that characterization in an irenic and culturally respectful way; they may be encountered in other countries besides America and in world missions where they have been introduced. However, the constant bombardment with such supposedly absolute claims, claims that for the most part insofar as the present study is concerned ultimately turn out to appear to be dictums molded by a good dose of presumption and lack of attention to detail, based primarily on proof-texting, had crept behind Theo's shield of faith. It is my hope that Theo—and all Spirit-empowered ministers, God willing—may be strengthened and instructed in their divine calling by whatever value my thoughts herein may offer.

Also, for those who might delve deeper and lead onward with respect to the issues addressed, I have provided a working Select Bibliography upon which students like Theo may build. I trust this may be helpful, informative, and profitable. It is designed to take students directly to the forefront of scholarship bearing on the important issues of the present study.

I would like to codedicate this project—with great admiration and respect—to the memory of Cora Fritsch, Alice Luce, Elize Scharten, and Elva Vanderbout, four Pentecostal pioneer women missionaries, evangelists, teachers, and pastors. The zeal, dedication, perseverance, and documented service of these Pentecostal ministers indeed leads by example for those who might be inspired to go to regions beyond. Some words from them may also serve as an appropriate and fitting foreword to my letter to Theo.

Alice Luce was a graduate of Cheltenham Ladies College, Cheltenham, England, which celebrated its 150th anniversary in 2004. She became an Anglican missionary to India, where she prayed for and received the gift of the Holy Spirit on February 10, 1910. Five years after her Spirit baptism (a contemporary Christian term adopted from the four Evangelists [Matt 3:11b; Mark 1:8; Luke 3:16; Acts 1:5; 11:16; John 1:33] for being baptized in the Holy Spirit or personally receiving the gift of the Spirit), she was ordained by the American Assemblies of God and pursued a divine calling to evangelistic and pastoral work in Monterrey, Mexico, and along the Rio Grande. She trained and vigorously supported indigenous gospel workers. During the Mexican Revolution, she returned to America and in 1926 founded what is now known as the Latin American Bible Institute and Theological Seminary, La Puente, California, developing curriculum and teaching at that school until her death in 1955. Her spiritually insightful literary output is inspiring as well as noteworthy, providing a window into her pastorally able missionary and educational work. She received a personal invitation to the coronation of Her Majesty Queen Elizabeth II in 1953.

Alice writes about her Mexican-American work to "a little band whose hearts God has touched, and who are ready to go forth to work for Him. I have been seeking to train them in the Word, and oh I wish you could see their eager faces, as they come to the night school after a hard day's work and drink in the Scriptures with the greatest vividity. . . . We shall have a baptismal service, when quite a number of the recent converts will confess their faith in Christ by being planted in the likeness of His death, and also a foot-washing service."[5] With respect to one convert, Miguel, she writes, "Much prayer, however, was made for him by the church here; and yesterday we received the joyful news that the day after returning to Los Indios the Lord baptized him with the Holy Spirit, and such a mighty revival has broken out that the young men are beg-

5. Luce, "Report of Mexican Work," *Weekly Evangel*, 13.

ging some of us to go down there and help them gather in the ripened sheaves. . . . Oh that the Lord would send us more workers—or to put it more accurately, oh that those whom He is calling would obey the call and come!"[6] Alice was motivated by the belief that the seed sown in faith will bear fruit in eternity. When the health department canceled her meetings for a month due to Spanish influenza, believing in the "Great Physician and His medicine," she reports that "Our time has been taken up more than ever in visiting the Christians and those seeking salvation, as well as praying with the sick. . . . Only one has been taken from us by death: a girl with tubercular tendency, who passed away very suddenly by influenza. Her last words were, 'The blood of Jesus is covering me,' and we rejoice that she is now safe with Him."[7]

Elize Scharten experienced the divine call as a teenager in Holland. Piet Klaver writes *in memoriam*: "Humanly speaking, she could have had an easy, lazy, and comfortable life. She had the means for this. But she chose the hard and difficult labor of being a pioneer. She did not spare herself. She was a hard worker and what she did herself, she expected from those who worked with her."[8] After an anointed and God-ordained ministry in China, we find the following testimony in her diary: "Everything lay behind me and much went through my soul. Yet, I knew I was in the will of the Lord. For some time I felt that my work in China was coming to an end. A part of my life was cut off with this departure. Thirty-four years of labor lay behind me and how many will there still be before me?"[9] She returned to her home country, The Netherlands, to the city

6. Luce, "Encouraging Report of Mexican Work," *Weekly Evangel*, 11.

7. Luce, "Mexican Work in California," *Christian Evangel*, 14.

8. van der Laan, "Beyond the Clouds," 354.

9. Ibid.

of Zeist (where, incidentally, I attended my first meeting of the European Pentecostal Theological Association) and she remained active there in door-to-door evangelism. She also preached throughout Holland.

Elize died on June 19, 1965. In 1990, a doctor from Groningen, Holland, visited Lijiang, China, on a medical mission. There he encountered an 83-year-old man who had been baptized by Elize when he was 25 years old. After insisting, the old man sang with a crackling voice, "*Yesu ling wuo, riri ling wuo,*" which translated means "Jesus leads me, leads me every day."[10] He told the doctor about the church services, the organ, and the bell that sounded to announce meetings, and then spoke the words of another prayer that he had learned from her.

Elva Vanderbout was called into the ministry at Bethel Temple Church in Los Angeles. She responded to a call for those who wanted to give their lives for the lost. She testified to having prayed at the altar, "I give myself to You! I will do what You ask me to do! I will go where you ask me to go! Oh God." She heard the still small voice, "Whom shall I send, and who will go for me?" From the depth of her heart she answered, "Here I am, send me."[11] Elva received a burden for the mountain people of the Philippines and began her ministry there on January 7, 1947. She ministered to the Tuding people, teaching, visiting homes, praying for the sick, and holding open-air services. Her passion and love for these mountain people and their children became well known and the Holy Spirit made her ministry effective. Sinners were converted and the healing of a crippled boy who crawled on the ground and who had ulcers is still remembered, as is that of a young girl who had been unable to hear or speak for twelve years and was instantly healed.

10. Ibid., 356.
11. Ma, "Elva Vanderbout," 74–75.

In a village in headhunter territory, an old man was carried by his friends from another village to the market place to hear. He was all bent over and could only walk on his hands and feet, like an animal. As Elva preached he instantly stood up and walked. In that meeting he accepted Christ as his savior, healer, and baptizer in the Holy Spirit. As a result of these meetings, believers in a village of 12,000 people built a church. Seven other churches were built among the people she loved. Elva also established orphanages for abandoned and neglected children. She died on October 16, 1990.

Cora Fritsch was called by the heavenly Jesus, upon hearing his words of Acts 1:8, to the remotest parts of the earth in the Orient. As the ship *Minnesota* pushed out of Puget Sound, Washington, she reflected about this experience, "'I am now sailing to the regions beyond where Jesus wants to use me and the glory of God is (surging) through my body again and again . . . best of all I felt the sunshine of my Savior's face beaming down upon me and the assurance that God is pleased with me.' Underneath her youthful exuberance rested a deep-seated commitment. Indeed, she knew that the Pentecostal baptism had empowered her for sharing the Good News."[12] Cora wrote home to family in another letter from Japan, "Oh! Dear ones, live closely to Jesus and some happy day I can see you all again. Oh! Dear papa, meet your Cora in Heaven, that is my dearest wish and prayer."[13] Cora later died in China, never having returned to the United States.

12. McGee, "Regions Beyond," 94.

13. Ibid., 82.

Introduction

D EAR THEO:
        I heartily applaud your desire to learn and to
consider; it is so important not to lose the desire to reflect.
I am also glad that you are seeking ministerial credentials
for future Pentecostal/Charismatic ministry. The thoughts
shared here on biblical interpretation and women's ministries are meant to help you fulfill your divine calling.

    We are grateful to have the written revelation of in-
spired scripture. Given this generous creative input from
the invisible God, it is wise to learn how to properly interpret these texts, which God's providence has preserved
for us. The occasional revelatory interpersonal spiritual gift
that is scripturally seasoned must of course be judged in
community, but does not require the same level of analytical
literary attention. The art, perhaps the science, of interpretation is much needed today. Proper interpretation is vital
for preachers who seriously desire to understand biblical
texts and their contexts. The Greeks' idea of contextual interpretation, using all levels of context, is expressed by their
word *hermeneia*. This idea was taken very seriously in the
Greco-Roman educational system that supported the rhetorical and literary culture within which the New Testament
documents were written.

    Unfortunately, we are currently faced with a lot of
noisy proof-texting and other noncontextual citing of snippets that support past ecclesiastical creeds and claims. This
appears to particularly be the case within "Bible-belt" zones
where we both live. At the Church of God Theological

Seminary I have encountered students from California and from Caribbean and South American countries who had never been exposed to claims of the cessation of women's ministries and who had never detected this cessation in their reading of scripture. Yet other students, predominately from Western countries, may have been overexposed to this approach. Even if one is not near a metaphorical "buckle on the Bible belt," one may be inundated with an intense proof-texting style of interpretation by some Evangelical Protestants that is imitative of the norms of past religious philosophy and male-dominated cultures. This approach may at times be overreactive to reasonable suggestions for positive change. It may also be unconcerned about both the communicative methods and the rhetorical culture of the first-century Greco-Roman world. While sincerely pious, it also may be less than adequately concerned about the very distinctive spiritual nature both of Jesus material and of Christian writings coming from that world.

To cite one example of that deportment from a historic Protestant sector of the United Kingdom, from the outset the Anglican Charismatic Renewal capably described itself as "a flowing tide of Christian believers" defined "by spiritual life, active and visible amongst them, by a strong sense of the power of God at work on earth (often in miraculous ways), by an upward-looking faith, by a claim of continuity with the early days of the apostolic church and an openness to the future, and by a preoccupation with God himself, even at the risk of seeming to lose touch with 'reality' of the more earthbound believers and unbelievers."[1] They pointed

---

1. Buchanan, et al., *Charismatic Movement*, 1 (parenthesis theirs). These sentiments somewhat echo those shared five years earlier by the editor of *Theological Renewal* who observed that "For many, such a direct renewing experience of the Spirit has meant a recovery of the assurance of faith." They had fallen "into a kind of legalism in which right doctrine took the place of living relationship to Christ,

out that what was "absolutely central" to the concerns of that movement was "the meeting of humankind and God, in particular the Spirit of God." In spite of their well-intended efforts, they were immediately attacked in a hurtful and presumptuous manner by an Evangelical theologian as being delusional and "deeply unbiblical."[2] This forceful attack was perceived as arrogant, no doubt unintended. Evidently, however, proper biblical interpretation was at the heart of the problem.

Following our conversations, dear Theo, I have felt impressed with the need to share a few thoughts about the value and method of proper biblical interpretation and about how the subject of women's ministries in our New Testament documents should be evaluated. This is quite essential at the present time, especially in the battle over interpretive method versus ideological proof-texting. I am

---

and the inculcation of orthodoxy was expected to do the work of the Holy Spirit in regenerating and sanctifying people. Debating theories of inspiration became a substitute for listening to God's word, and reading books about him took the place of praying to him" (Smail, "Theology of Renewal," 2).

2. A journal with ties to traditional Anglicanism, *Chm*, published two tandem articles suggesting "delusion" and a "deeply unbiblical" nature of the Renewal, wherein it was dubbed as nothing more than a "false restoration" of "sign-gifts." For discussion of this instructive episode and a response to James I. Packer's articles—a response rejected by *Chm*—in light of both what New Testament writers themselves actually say and the reasonable correlation of their Spirit-language with contemporary Christian experience, cf. Elbert, "Charismatic Movement," *passim*.

The quite illuminating point, with respect to our concern here relative to a "Bible-belt" style of ideological interpretation, is that the intended squelching effect of this sort of harsh and presuppositionally based criticism from the proof-texting theological perspective of modern cessationism appears to have had no long-term effect whatever. The Renewal throughout the United Kingdom continues to blossom, cf. Steven, *Worship in the Spirit*.

hopeful that as your ministry continues to develop the following introductory thoughts, and what follows, may be useful to you.

First, in "Bible-belt" zones, if I might employ this metaphor to identify a less than satisfactory, snippety style of determining a biblical author's intended meaning, it could be posited that there may exist an ingrained tendency—principally among various Evangelical groups, but certainly not all—to make bold and textually untested and unconsidered claims based on proof-texting. This technique appears to be employed to validate claims of past tradition that are rightly being called into question. However, the religious norms of some today, no matter in what country they may reside, do not necessarily fit either the literary communicative practice or the very distinctive *Christian* outlook of the New Testament writers, so that the subordination of New Testament thought to contemporary cultural or secular traditions may not be the way forward.

Now, let me follow this observation by noting that Evangelical Protestants throughout the world are fine people. The evangelistic-minded global Pentecostal and international Charismatic Renewal movements share, in part, an overlapping tradition with them. So here I am not by any means trying to raise negative criticism of Evangelicals within world Christendom. However, it does seem necessary to address the influential, overly ambitious claims and insufficiently examined assertions of some. The majority in these Evangelical Protestant traditions are simply repeating in good faith what they have been led to believe, without any further consideration. However, because these claims may appear unreflective and dogmatic in nature, not the product of any real sense of contextual interpretation of New Testament texts, they warrant further comment. In this sometimes intense climate of proof-texting one simply grabs a fragment of a text that suits the defense of ingrained dogma, eliminating the context of a writer's overall contextual thought. Then, the fragment is advanced as "biblical truth." It is not unusual to observe that the fragmentary noncontextual thought eventually becomes promoted as absolute, sometimes by ministers and scholars who, even in their haste, should know better.

By "absolute" I mean that it is simply repeated over and over and over, cloned without question or investigation, until it becomes absolutely undoubtable. Anyone who doubts such dubious proof-texted claims might be considered fringy, of minimal status, of "questionable orthodoxy," one who is "ideologically inappropriate," one who is outside the camp, who, if possible, might be cast out. These terms are even employed by some to sweepingly describe the majority of world Christendom that is neither Roman Catholic nor Orthodox, that is, to describe all those who believe in personally receiving the gift of the Holy Spirit, in the practice of interpersonal spiritual gifts, and in the support of women's ministries—Spirit-giftedness and divine calling eliminated by a theory of cessation in the "apostolic-age" hermeneutic of historic Protestantism. So, dear Theo, we live in a semantically confusing and serious time in which capable biblical exegesis and hermeneutics are very much needed, along with wisdom to understand how interpretive method impacts tradition. If you are dubbed with these "Bible-belt" type terms please let me assure you that you are in good company, along with Cora Fritsch, Alice Luce, Elize Scharten, and Elva Vanderbout, for example.

Since the supposed absoluteness of such "biblical truth"—information extracted from its context and established primarily by proof-texting—becomes, for some, beyond question, it may eventually rival the Bible itself within this interpretive culture. Now the Bible is a very distinguished literary book, a book of credible historicity and truthfulness; it does not deserve to be subjected to such haphazard interpretive tactics. Nevertheless, such poorly extracted "truth" may become revered and rationalized as the "word of God." However, when tradition becomes endowed with an overinflated interpretive authority it does not deserve, the thoughtful communication of New Testament writers may be left behind. Although the Fourth Gospel says that Jesus himself is the "Word of God" (John 1:1), this preeminent concept seems underplayed. Instead, an overemphasis gradually accrues to such proof-texted tradition and it evolves into an absolute standard. The extracted fragment eventually becomes a "word" almost coequal to Jesus and is assimilated as essentially divine. Instead of worshiping God, the proof-texted and undoubted fragment may be coequally worshipped. It is put in a collection of doctrines, to be imprinted and reimprinted on the minds of hearers. Ministers focus on what is doctrinally acceptable and keep the tradition of proof-texting alive. This performance reminds me of the following lines from John Greenleaf Whittier's poem, "The Eternal Goodness":

> But still my human hands are weak
> To hold your iron creeds:
> Against the words ye bid me speak
> My heart within me pleads. . . .
> I walk with bare, hushed feet the ground
> Ye tread with boldness shod;
> I dare not fix with mete and bound
> The love and power of God.

Eventually, God, who gives free will to those who might unintentionally participate in the misleading indoctrination of others, could be understood historically as tiring of it and as bringing forth a new development. In his time, at the beginning of the twentieth century, a new faith tradition bursts upon the world. The primal narrative of that birth is that of an oppressed people yearning for and receiving emancipation from an oppressive empire. Global Pentecostalism was and is birthed out of the hungering cries of people who desired to see, to glimpse, the glory of God. Much that is orthodox is alive and well, but some of it is dead and dead orthodoxy can hide the face of God from the humble, the contrite, and the broken. From within the oppressive empire God heard the cries of these people and filled their empty hearts with his fire. Even now, lament and desire to seek for the living God, to "pray through,"[3] is a part of the primal identity of the Pentecostal and Neo-Pentecostal Renewal.

This is the time in which we now live, dear Theo—the time of global Pentecostalism and international Charismatic Renewal as a major developing sector of world Christendom—wherein scripture is considered as a connected and cohesive grand narrative which should be read sensitively. The proof-texting culture of some within a distinguished Evangelical Protestant faith tradition is now in a lively battle with an improved approach to understanding biblical texts, an approach that emphasizes levels of context and the probable intention of an author and the original meaning in scriptural revelation. There is a new attitude afoot that does not simply want to uncritically affirm century-old teachings and dogmatic convictions, but one that seeks fresh views on biblical traditions and raises new questions about the personhood and workings of the Holy Spirit. For example, this new exploration is reflected in ideas that the Holy Spirit is one person in many persons and that the first Jerusalem Pentecost, in ever-increasing concentric circles "in Jerusalem and in all Judea and Samaria and to the end of the earth" (Acts 1:8), reveals the normative and fundamental profile of the covenantal presence of God with

3. McQueen, "Appropriation," 77; Land, "Pentecostal Spirituality as Vision," *passim.*

his people that is valid for all times and determines their subsequent history.[4] It may be suggested that we are living in a time when God is making visible via the Christian community his prophetic promise about Jesus (Acts 1:4–5) and the fullness of the Spirit of Christ.

Second, this new movement of Renewal is reevaluating some past uncritical assertions. It begins a new quest for finding out what New Testament authors mean and directly challenges an artificially imposed temporal chasm between original and later readers. What do these authors actually think? To find out, an interpretive procedure sensitive to literary cohesion and connectivity of thought finds initial appreciation and employment. The proof-texting component within past Evangelical Protestant tradition, or any faith tradition, can never be acknowledged as being a credible interpretive procedure, no matter how influential. Proof-texting and the erasure and elimination of context must be subjected to question. Marginalization of a New Testament author's thought in order to make that author conform to an established belief system is a procedure that must be challenged.

For example, the writer of Luke-Acts was not a Calvinist and did not equate inspired, nonrational, prophetic speech or glossolalia with preaching the Gospel. This is something that Calvinism imposed on New Testament texts and then proof-texted them accordingly. I say this as an admirer of a goodly portion of Calvin's ministry and of the fact that he asked to be buried in an unmarked grave, although a few of his misguided, quasi-philosophical presuppositions about a supposed "apostolic age" left a lasting misimpression upon some. Additionally, within the contemporary Renewal, it is the Holy Spirit, the inspirer, leader, and guide, who is experientially discerned—via personal and sometimes communal

4. Mühlen, *Kirche wächst von innen*, 199.

discernment beyond the rational intellectual assent—as being personally interested in and concerned with contemporary readers finding out what biblical texts mean and what their authors intended to communicate. Of course, this quest for interpretive acumen is a fine and deserving literary interest that invites universal participation. I am simply saying that within the international Charismatic Renewal and global Pentecostalism the Holy Spirit is detected, not just theologically assumed, as expressing a keen and active personal interest in understanding biblical texts aright. Of course I realize that this statement lacks exact exemplarity that would be appropriate in a private conversation and that it is subject to judgment.

Third, this more sensitive interpretive procedure has returned in some respects to the ancient literary practice of affording an intelligent writer, including New Testament writers, the credibility of having commonsensical continuity of thought. This means that a writer's thought on a particular topic or subject that he mentions or seriously addresses must be engaged with an interpretive process that considers the *entirety* of his thoughts. Proof-texting and fragmentary extractions are out; context(s) and serious reflection about an author's intended meaning are in. New schools are built. A new generation of ministers is trained. Evangelization of the world is renewed. But the old ways live on—particularly in "Bible-belt" zones of any geographical location, where generations there may have been taught to read the Bible via proof-texting and memorization of supposed absolutes that are selected to fit past doctrine. Of course real *storytime* and *spacetime* actualities exist as objective truth, for example "God is love" and "Jesus is a savior."

Other claims sound absolute, like for example "Pentecost was, like osmosis, 'once for all'," "Jesus' instruction to pray for the gift of the Holy Spirit has ceased," "Women today cannot speak in church," and "Paul's instruction to seek interpersonal spiritual gifts has ceased." Here there is a strong difference of opinion as to whether these dictums reflect New Testament thought, and the way forward is to get back to interpretive method instead of relying on quick and dogmatic claims. I agree with Kurz, that "Since God has chosen to reveal his message in the words of men, complete with the limitations of those words, we have no recourse but to use the human talents and resources which God has given us, along with the guidance of his Spirit, to study the human aspects of his word and discover how it is to be applied to our own times."[5] Doctrine should be examined and subjected to critical reflection. Insufficiently examined dogma may have gradually emerged historically in various locations as a cultural paradigm in and of itself and, through repetition, has perhaps sometimes become so paramount that it might appear to even replace love itself, replace the divine will, replace the divine calling, and, not least of all, actually replace and obscure what New Testament writers themselves had in mind for their original readers—and their anticipated future readers—to understand.

In what follows I would like to offer some important and practical examples from the New Testament that I believe serve to illustrate and document these three aforementioned points.

---

5. Kurz, "Inspiration and Origins," 58.

1

The Fourth Gospel
and Related Observations

JOHN 3:16 can and should be used absolutely, as in a gospel tract, to tell sinners what God is like. John 3:16–21 also can and should be preached contextually to believer-disciples to reinforce Christian faith. John 7:39, "But this he spoke about the Spirit, whom those who believed in him were to receive; for the Spirit had not yet been (given), because Jesus was not yet glorified," however, needs more explanatory context because it assumes connective elements and an informed original readership. While it is sometimes difficult to distinguish between narration and authorial commentary, at John 7:39 the intentional commentary is obvious. Here we have a precise and intrusive comment by the author to explain what the words of Jesus actually mean. The author probably considers this to be an important clarification of the timing of an event in which believers were to participate. Given that in the Fourth Gospel these narrative asides are employed over a hundred times for several purposes, such as clarifying thoughts of characters, we must assume that the author expected John 7:39 to be taken seriously.

It could be suggested that the reason a major prophecy by a significant character (John the Baptist) about the central character (Jesus), describing a forthcoming spiritual phenomenon to be initiated by the central character and identified as a "baptism in the Holy Spirit" (John 1:33), appears somewhat underdeveloped in the Fourth Gospel—to modern rhetorical eyes—is not because this Spirit-language was *not* being used in early Christianity, but rather because it *was* being actively used. To leave out what was already well-understood for reasons of conciseness was a practical narrative-rhetorical tactic functioning in first-century Greco-Roman education that goes back to Homer. Accordingly, John could easily expect his original readers to readily grasp the connection between 1:33 and 7:39 and to recognize that what is being narrated here is speaking to readers' own personal experiences of Spirit-reception currently described as a baptism in the Holy Spirit by the now heavenly Jesus. Perhaps this may be more reasonable—from a Greco-Roman rhetorical perspective—than assuming that the language from Jesus tradition at John 1:33 and 7:39 was not being used in early Christianity.

Further, an assumption of readers' own Spirit-reception is coherent with the claims about the various detectable spiritual phenomena the Spirit will initiate beyond narrative time (John 14:16–17, 26; 15:26; 16:13–14). These unusual phenomena are best understood as being both plausible and believable to original active readers. On my reading these spiritual phenomena are activities of the Holy Spirit that readers are expected to be familiar with—activities stemming from their own baptism in the Holy Spirit by the heavenly Jesus. As to authorial intention, these spiritual events are expected to be plausible and believable not just because these future phenomena are claimed to exist due to the fact that they are described in *storytime*, but because they are expected by the author to be genuinely understood to exist experientially by an active readership in *spacetime*.

When preaching from the Fourth Gospel today, hearers need both connective and immediate context when that preaching includes John 7:39. The Spirit-Paraclete, sent by the Father to counterbalance the departure of the earthly Jesus (John 14:16–17, 25–26; 15:26–27; 16:7–15), now mediates the presence of the heavenly Jesus. The didactic and other revelatory functions of the Spirit, granted at the Lord's discretion, provide recognizable guidance and encouragement within the lives of those who believe that Jesus is the Christ, the son of God. We need to be expecting these revelatory activities of the Spirit of truth and looking forward to their productive utilization. When heaven is silent, we may take comfort in the reign and rule of the soon coming king.

Participants in the proof-texting tradition of the sixteenth century onward generally tended to ignore or marginalize John 7:39 in its narrative and New Testament context. Phenomena of this miraculous nature were confined to an "apostolic age." John 7:39, an editorial clarification by an intelligent author, thus may become a nontext. Scholars, on the other hand, always realized that the passage spoke of something real in original reader's lives, but in general have not explored a probable connection of the futurity of believers receiving the Spirit (7:39a) with the foregrounded prophecy of Jesus baptizing in the Spirit (1:33b), also in the future.[1] New "narrative exploration," as suggested by Thomas, is in order.[2] In any case, within the rhetorical culture of the first-century Greco-Roman world, a literary digression like John 7:39, which offered an important clarification of meaning, was understood to have a definite purpose. Active readers in that world who interacted with

1. Porsch's straightforward observation on "Das >Noch-nicht< des Geistes" of 7:39b, illustrates the need for exploration in this regard, namely that "Die Feststellung »denn noch war nicht Pneuma« (V.39b) soll die vorhergehende Aussage erklären und begründen, daß den Geist erst die bereits (in der Zunkunft) Gläubiggewordenen empfangen werden (V.39a)," *Pneuma und Wort*, 65.

2. Thomas, "Spirit in the Fourth Gospel."

a literary text perked up their ears. They became curious. A predictive digression by a respected author about his central character was duly perceived as no idle or simplistic tactic. Such a literary device was knowingly placed in a text to engage the attention of active—not passive—readers, readers who would talk back to a text, ask questions, and interpret according to their own experience and contemporary expression of that experience.

John 7:39 could first be designed to directly engage the experience of active Greco-Roman literary-minded readers, referring to an experience from the heavenly Jesus that they would already understand, encouraging them to read the text of the Fourth Gospel in light of that experience. Active readers would probably not just be looking for what this editorial clue might do for understanding the experience of characters in the story of the text itself, like John 20:19–23, which because of its limited nature would probably not be taken as a textually internal fit to 7:39. In terms of the contemporary narrative-rhetorical practice of characterization/personification it would be an excessively narrow outcome for 1:33 and 7:39. Further, since active readers would need no help to work backwards from this later scene to earlier material, they could reasonably expect the guidance from 7:39 to refer to something beyond the text, to an experience beyond narrative time. Believers other than those immediately in view in the text itself are carefully mentioned as a priority of the earthly Jesus (John 17:20; 20:29). Active readers might well ask what 7:39 could be intended to do for their reading of this document in light of their own Christian experience, knowledge, and tradition, based on preaching, teaching, and previous presentations of Jesus material (as cited in Luke 1:1) with which they were acquainted. So, John 7:39 surely appears originally designed to stimulate interest for active readers. It is a narrative aside worthy of serious consideration and would resonate with readers who already employed the descriptive

Spirit-reception language of John's narratively foregrounded prophecy in their own engagement with the heavenly Jesus and the Holy Spirit.

Nevertheless, Christians today who take an active and serious interest in the narrative explanation or digression found in John 7:39, both with respect to contemporary Christian experience and to experience and descriptive information probably functioning among original readers of the Fourth Gospel, may not be welcomed into the interpretive conversation of some. Those who would employ 7:39 as a part of their ministry today with respect to predictive strands of the Fourth Gospel that apparently stem from the experience described there and from other parts of the New Testament might be placed under a cloud of suspicion by some for raising new possibilities. To this mindset, John 3:3 is still in effect, but John 7:39 must surely fade away. For later readers of this document, its literary, theological, and pneumatological import must cease. The fact that 7:39 is foregrounded by an important prophecy (John 1:33) about the ministry of Jesus—the heavenly Jesus as far as active original readers are concerned—may be ignored within wider New Testament contexts. The issue that a significant prophecy about Jesus' future ministry of baptizing in the Holy Spirit (1:33) does not seem to readily fit the event described in John 20:19–23 for a select few, and that the writer may have wanted to help readers avoid that conclusion by an insightful digression, is an issue that passively fades away.

So, dear Theo, if you find that your voice cannot be given a hearing within the interpretive conversation, please allow me to suggest that you ask yourself this question: "What would the New Testament writers do if they were in my place today?" As you yield yourself to Jesus and seek to be pleasing and productive in his sight, I expect that you will be given an appropriate answer. The depths of the narrative presentation of the insightful and competent author of the Fourth Gospel will never cease to be explored. This great theological composition deserves our utmost respect. A style of chasmal and snippety interpretation loaded with "apostolic-age" presuppositions cannot really do justice to the witness of the beloved disciple.

Also, there may be implications to be drawn from the possibility that John 7:39 was penned by the same person as the John of Acts 1:13; 8:14–15, certainly a distinct historical probability that cannot be overlooked. The experiential statements in the Fourth Gospel about what realities the Holy Spirit will actually initiate within believers who receive the Spirit (like John 14:16–17, 26; 15:26; 16:13) cannot just be spiritualized as in the aforementioned Calvinistic equation of New Testament prophecy with preaching in general. The precise teaching function of the Johannine *chrisma*, translated as "anointing" or "unction" and as "Salbung" in German and "oints" from "oindre" in French (1 John 2:20, 27), should also not be spiritualized, equated with reading, or confined to an "apostolic age." On the contrary, it should continue to be explored on its own merits based on how it is described, given that original readers were expected to understand its function. These texts, which descriptively reveal interesting and precise revelatory experiences—details that I suggest are related to the same communicative and rhetorical motivation for deliberately inserting John 7:39 into the narrative—may be duly venerated as scripture by some, but then interest in the potential revelatory participation that these texts convey may be squelched, inappropriately confined to characters in the Fourth Gospel itself, or restricted to an original readership. Such a chasmal and disruptive presumption between original and later readers—obviously at odds with any reasonable understanding of authorial intention—seems excessively contemporary, not rooted in the character of Christian faith as a thinking faith that is duly attentive to Greco-Roman narrative-rhetorical constructs, to preceding classical literary constructs, and to a serious consideration of the intention of intelligent first-century Christian authors.

Along a similar historical vein, in Evangelical Protestant tradition the book of Acts itself was reduced by some to mere history, supposedly entombed in an "apostolic age," so what happens in this narrative, on this presupposition, is not only unwanted by some contemporary readers entrenched in the proof-texting tradition of "apostolic-age" interpretation, but also simply immaterial. Preaching from Acts, in this vein, would properly focus on points of morality or ethics; the theological and pneumatological significance of the narrative is either marginalized or extinguished. With rare exceptions, the modern dispensational/cessationist tradition stemming from a historic concretization of "apostolic-age" hermeneutics assisted by the Reformation usually either insists or implies that "Pentecost can never be repeated." Luke appears to disagree, but that is overridden because Luke and his characters, both male and female, are encapsulated in an artificial, extra-biblical epoch and are not afforded a voice. Women, like Philip's prophesying daughters, are especially targeted for cessation. What happens in the *storytime* of Acts—with respect to characterization of Peter, John, Philip, Philip's daughters, Paul, Priscilla, and Apollos—is immaterial to *spacetime* actuality today, an attitude strangely incongruous with apparent authorial intent toward Luke's original reader (Theophilus). Luke's thought is reinterpreted accordingly so that his writing appears to fit this seemingly strange dogma of chasmal separation that, historically, can be observed to mutate over the past two centuries within Evangelical Protestant tradition to increasing complexity by its continuous embellishment.

Peter's apparent projection of the gift of the Holy Spirit beyond narrative time at the end of his sermon in Acts 2, a gift that in ancient literary personification and among original, rhetorically minded, active readers would be construed as the same gift that Peter himself just received (Acts 2:38c–39), is discounted in favor of repeating Calvin's self-serving dictum that this does not apply to us today. I will return to this point later in more detail, but it looks like the John of Acts 1:13–14 and of Acts 8 could not have believed this particular dictum, otherwise why would he travel to Samaria to minister the gift of the Holy Spirit to baptized believers? In fact, again, the "apostolic-age" style of proof-texting and its frequent, narratively incoherent interpretations takes little recognition of the examples and precedents of Spirit-reception in Luke-Acts as adequately characterized by Peter, John, and Philip (Acts 8:14–17), Ananias and Paul (Acts 9:17), and by Paul's question in the context of strengthening disciple-believers (Acts 19:2a), an easily understandable question very much in keeping with the syntax of Luke's composition of questions. The subject of Spirit-reception is one that Jesus introduces as a matter of prayer to disciples in Luke 11:5–13, which Luke carefully then extends from Luke 24:49 on into his second book prepared for Theophilus (Luke 1:3; Acts 1:1), a believer who might have previously expressed an interest to Luke as to what expectations he should have regarding his own interest in Spirit-reception. Luke certainly writes as if he has a real person before his mind's eye, a person who will understand him.

Nevertheless, Luke 11:5–13 is often unacknowledged as even being a part of Jesus' teaching on prayer. Traditionally, it is not included in the "Lord's Prayer" or in the "Our Father." Nevertheless, it is astutely foregrounded by an important prophecy (Luke 3:16) of which the earthly Jesus appears narratively to be quite aware in his teaching on prayer. (Note that Mark and Matthew cite John the Baptist's prophecy, but then they drop it from the story line, perhaps, I suggest, because of known familiarity on the part of their readership and not because they would otherwise ignore such an important narrative element and historical component of Christian tradition.) Given Luke's rhetorical development of this topic from John's prophecy, it is difficult to disconnect both Luke 3:16 and 11:13 from Luke 24:49, although in a part of Protestant interpretive tradition this kind of incohesive move is often taken. Here, I suggest, we see how allegiance to past cessationistic elements of a faith tradition can override what an intelligent author probably intended for Theophilus to readily grasp by narrative repetition and attention to contextual development. It is fair to say that Luke's evident interest in fulfillment of prophecy as a literary and narrative-rhetorical theme, based on John the Baptist's prophecy that Jesus will baptize in the Holy Spirit, is ignored in an "Evangelical Historical Critical Method" of interpretation that, I argue, might best be replaced with a "Theologically and Pneumatologically Sensitive Narrative-Critical Rhetorical Method."

2

First Corinthians and Related Observations

FIRST CORINTHIANS 11:5a, "But every woman praying or prophesying with the head uncovered (or unveiled, *akatakaluptō*, disgraces her head," on its own is quite understandable. Paul believes women will and should prophesy, God willing, if their heads are covered in a socially acceptable manner. In many worship settings today in Western and other countries, head coverings of some sort are understood to be an unrequired part of a past culture and the participation of women who minister in prophecy is not tied to the cultural constraints of a past time or place. However, in many Orthodox churches today women do wear veils and this tradition is to be respected. In any event, within an interpretive style of proof-texting that requires a temporal chasm between the original and all later readers of the New Testament, First Corinthians 11:5a is of little interest. Many charisms and revelatory activities of the Spirit are eliminated by the presumption of this temporal chasm.

This unexamined presumption—that all interpersonal spiritual gifts unnatural in appearance were supposedly removed from the province of Christendom by a divine edict when the New Testament documents were finished—is in need of reappraisal, in spite of a distinctive dispensational/cessationistic "interpretation" of First Corinthians 13:10, in which "that which is perfect" is theoretically transformed into the "canon of Scripture." When the last ink dried on the last papyrus leaf or scroll of a New Testament document that was destined to be preserved, "that which is perfect" supposedly appeared and Christians—Paul including his readers and not confining his remarks to himself—could from then on see face-to-face and know as we are known.

Some Evangelicals have misled readers of their various study Bibles with this unthoughtful tactic for years. Grammatical ploys cannot resolve this obvious contextual conflict and the misleading of many continues unabated. However, when it was belatedly realized by some that this claim did not make sense, "the perfect" of First Corinthians 13:10 was reinvented to be a contextually disembodied and undefined intermediate epochal point in church history between the first century and today. Arbitrarily selected charisms would supposedly cease then and supposedly right doctrine could be preserved, even though the immediate context of Paul's thought clearly implies that when "that which is perfect" appears Christians will see face-to-face and fully understand as we are now understood or known.

All of this takes little notice of the substantial critical commentary tradition on First Corinthians which is unanimous in contextually identifying "that which is perfect" (*to teleion*, 13:10) with the return of Christ,[1] *not* with written

---

1. It is only fitting here to make mention of scholars whose critical commentaries may be consulted with appreciation, all of whom are found to consistently reach the aforementioned contextual interpretation of Paul's *to teleion* at 13:10 and rightly understand him there as calling attention to the termination of the *charismata* (or interpersonal spiritual gifts) at the end, when Christians will see face-to-face, on the day of the Lord Jesus Christ (1 Cor 1:8): E. Bernard Allo, Philipp Bachmann, Charles K. Barrett, Wilhelm Bousset, Frederick F. Bruce, Hans Conzelmann, Gordon D. Fee, Jean Héring, Georg Heinrici, Joseph Huby, Jacob Kremer, Otto Kuss, Friedrich Lang, Hans Lietzmann, Andreas Lindemann, Helmut Merklein/ Markis Gielen, Heinrich A. W. Meyer, Werner Meyer, William

documents or another dubious extrabiblical epoch. It also takes little notice of quality scholarship from within the Reformed tradition itself. Klaas Runia, who taught practical theology for twenty years at the Theological University of the *Gereformeerde Kerke* (Reformed Churches) in Kampen, The Netherlands, won great respect for his contributions to theology and the life of the church. His timely study on "Gifts of the Spirit" rightly urged an interpretive path respectful of Scripture in coincidence with the critical commentators and away from uncritical Calvinistic tradition in misidentifying "the perfect" (*to teleion*, 13:10) with the Bible.[2] In his recent work, *Op zoek naar de Geest* (*On the Search for the Spirit*), Runia builds on his "Gifts" and expands positively on fellow Dutch Reformed scholar Herman Ridderbos' view that "It is very well possible, that the Spirit also in our time wants to bring the church alive by means of certain breakthroughs and outpourings of gifts. I think we should pray for it, than turn against it."[3]

Nevertheless, First Corinthians 13:10 remains a major proof-texting passage for the modern dispensational/cessationistic mindset and its collection of absolute claims. According to this worldview, this extracted excerpt teaches that when God saw that the Bible's last word was written, he initiated a new epoch wherein interpersonal spiritual gifts—operations of the Holy Spirit ministering through a Christian to another person that would appear to humankind as beyond the natural realm— were withdrawn. These were thereby sealed off from the participation of all

---

Orr/James Walther, Franz Ortkemper, Archibald Robertson/Alfred Plummer, Adolf Schlatter, Paul W. Schmiedel, Wolfgang Schrage, Christophe Senft, Marion L. Soards, August Strobel, Johannes Weiss, Heinz-Dietrich Wendland, and Christian Wolff.

2. Runia, "Gifts of the Spirit," *passim*.

3. Runia, *Op zoek naar de Geest*, 51. I am grateful to Melody-Joy Wassmer for her translation.

future New Testament believers by divine edict and forever encapsulated or casketed in a supposed "apostolic age." This fantastic claim is extracted from this textual fragment and touted as absolute in a spate of study Bibles presented as seemingly authoritative, piously promoting this claim as supportive of other artificial procedures that have influenced millions of unsuspecting readers.[4] With all due respect, at least the appearance of subterfuge is difficult to avoid. In the Bible Belt proper the market for this publishing industry represents a very lucrative business.

What is unfortunately overlooked in this arbitrary voiding of the concept of interpersonal spiritual giftedness is the truncation of a wonderful dimension of Paul's concept of love.[5] The interpersonal sharing or transmission of a concrete grace under the loving direction of the Holy Spirit represents an interweaving of an uplifting and mutually edifying revelatory process, an operation of the Spirit that I am sure Paul would not want to be terminated. I suspect he would feel that such an extinguishment via presuppositional and tenuous theoretical speculation would be quite unwarranted. Nevertheless, under an imposed system guaranteeing that a host of activities of the Holy Spirit cannot occur beyond this chasmal cutoff, or beyond any suitable epochal artifice that could be exploited to satisfy the completed perfection or maturity of all believers before they see face-to-face, it seems permissible to yank texts out of context anywhere at will and apply cessationistic surgery to them in order to "make them fit."

---

4. The deleterious overall effects of a scheme wherein "the perfect" (*to teleion*, 1 Cor 13:10) is inventively morphed into something dramatically against Paul's evident contextual thinking, befitting the ideology of the modern dispensational/cessationistic worldview, is well addressed by Prosser, *Dispensationalist Eschatology*.

5. Cf. Lyonnet, "*Agape* et charismes selon 1 Cor 12, 31."

A case in point is First Corinthians 11:5a. The editors and authors of study Bibles purporting this worldview strongly express the view that the spiritual experience represented by texts like 11:5a is then duly voided. According to this contemporary religious culture, it would even be childish to pursue such experience. In other words, this scenario explicitly demands that experience represented by such a text, like 11:5a, is something that cannot happen in later readers' lives. The proponents of this procedure do not want this or any similar revelatory experience for interpersonal edification to happen to them or to anybody else. The make-it-fit interpretive procedure is king. It dominates all. Here, prophesying women, with experience that contains the miraculous or the supernatural, are persons not to be considered as relevant after being walled off in an "apostolic age." Yet, such women appear to be confined to a past epoch of tight temporal boundaries by little more than willful supposition. It is as if prophesying women (and men) do not fit the contemporary doctrinal purity of some and are thus dismissed from vital participation in the life and work of the church as understood by Paul. With all due respect, we have to call a spade a spade and bring this into question.

While it is difficult to believe that the aforementioned truncating maneuvers are motivated by the thinking expressed by *any* New Testament writer, this erasure is nevertheless justified to laypersons by claiming that at some moment after Paul wrote about Christian experience of prophetic-type giftedness, this and other operations of the Holy Spirit useful to the church were scheduled for elimination by a divine edict. While revelatory giftedness is supposedly terminated, the quasi-revelation of that ecclesiastically sanctioned elimination of spiritual giftedness is validated or confirmed by a proof-texting style of chasm-oriented interpretation. First Corinthians 11:5a is thusly erased.

While this prophetic experience and these persons that are described here by Paul within New Testament Christianity do not fit into some Evangelical Protestant doctrine and political power, should such quick and dogmatic claims be accepted? As striking as it may seem to observers today, the propagation of these odd-sounding cessationistic ideas and their unexamined presuppositional corollaries continues amongst its adherents without substantive analysis. This relatively uncontested scheme has been in pamphlets, in study Bibles, and on the radio and television for years, First Corinthians 13:10 being contextually misused as a bastion of scripture reading via the imposition of extra-biblical epochs. It may be fair to say, with all due respect, that scientific curiosity is not a hallmark of this long-standing paleoreformed tradition.

The Christian prophetesses of First Corinthians 11:5a, whose gifts of inspired speech explicitly included the teaching and building up of the congregation (1 Cor 14:3, 5), are thus forgotten. Nevertheless, for those who would remember, along with First Corinthians 14:39a, "So as, my brethren, be eager (or earnestly desire) to prophesy," we might take note of Paul's other gender-neutral imperatives in this specific regard (1 Thess 5:19–20; 1 Cor 12:31a; 14:1). Among some, however, Paul's instructions pertaining to prophetic ministry seem never to surface on "proper" preachers' lips in "Bible-belt" zones. Miraculous prophetic inspiration and prophetic revelation of any sort should not occur and is banned. Paul's thought is discarded. First Corinthians 11:5a is far removed from the collection of absolute claims that function as "biblical truth" in these zones to propagate the traditions of modern cessationism. It is not in catechisms or voiced in Sunday schools concerned about "what we believe." It is not a part of knowledge that is relevant to the only acceptable doctrine. It is not gleaned from proof-texting and presented as a ministry to seek or imitate.

Some Evangelical Protestants keep it under a total eclipse. Their ministers ignore it. Their students do not learn it. Their students do not ask "How do we know?" and "Why do we believe?" The significance of First Corinthians 11:5a for Paul's thought and mission-praxis is lost to fanciful reinterpretation and exaggeration under the sway of a great interpretive and ideological gulf imposed between Paul's original readers and all his later readers.

One recent study Bible invents a twenty-first century Calvinistic Paul at First Corinthians 11:5a who, in speaking of women who pray or prophesy, according to the explanation of what this particular passage means, is claimed to be stating explicitly here "that women are not to lead or speak in the services of the church, but they may pray and proclaim the truth to unbelievers, as well as teaching children."[6] Does Paul actually say *any* of this? Or, is this just pious rewriting to "make it fit"? In this incongruous scenario, if adult male unbelievers were to be converted, then women's ministries must cease, lest they supposedly be guilty of demeaning authoritarianism and ideological inappropriateness by teaching or preaching to Christian men. In this incongruous scenario, women are prohibited from teaching or preaching to Christian men in colleges, seminaries, and on the mission field. Could it be presumptuous to insist that the Holy Spirit supports or approves of this sexist treatment of Christian women? Such anti-Pauline imposition of the contemporary subcultural practice of some upon this text, while grossly distorting and apparently paying no attention to what Paul actually writes here, may well be cloned and further misused by religious opinion-makers as "proof" of the true "biblical" nature of unexamined dictums to which they have grown accustomed. What the Bible *says*, without due regard for what its authors *meant*,

6. MacArthur, *1 Corinthians*, 69.

will be the spin. Instead, such anti-Pauline imposition should be robustly questioned for the misleading secular embellishment that it actually is. The real Paul, the suffering charismatic apostle, missionary, and writer of occasional letters, appreciated the spiritual giftedness of all those in Christ Jesus and had a respectful working relationship with Christian women ministers, as this present study attempts to demonstrate. Paul's collaboration with them is unrelated to the misrepresentative interpretive chaos of MacArthur's unabashed proof-texting.

Nevertheless, in God's time, at the beginning of the twentieth century, a new, more reflective and considerate strategy for understanding New Testament thought arrives. It arrives, strangely, not from the erudite or academic elite, but from among the simple and the oppressed with a deep hunger for God. While there are blunders and mistakes within human weakness, with little help being offered by modern cessationistic protagonists other than to attempt to stifle new ideas, insights, and discoveries, much theological and biblical study from a different presuppositional angle is accomplished. As to the inevitable excesses within human weakness that can accompany new discoveries, I wonder if any of them might compare to the grand theology of cessationistic speculation sometimes exhibited by Calvin and some of his hermeneutical descendants, an interpretive excess amply illustrated by the Geneva Reformer in his commentary on Acts 2:38, "He (Peter) promises them the same gift (*eiusdem doni*) of the Spirit of which they saw an example in the diversity of tongues (*linguarum diuersitate*). Therefore this does not exactly apply to us. For since it was by the inauguration of his kingdom that Christ meant to set forth miracles, they lasted only for a time; but because the visible graces which the Lord distributed to his own mirrored forth that Christ was the giver of the Spirit, the words of Peter—'You shall receive the gift of the Holy Spirit (*ac-*

cipietis donum Spiritus)'—apply in a measure to the whole Church."[7] While Calvin and his hermeneutical descendants are devout, their claim of chasmal separation is exegetically presumptuous, nonliterary in origin, and difficult to attach to biblical texts.

Neither the writer of Luke-Acts nor any other New Testament author says or even suggests *any* of this "not exactly applying to us" theory, a culturally accommodating and politically helpful theory that Calvin advances and pronounces as fact. Calvin rightly recognizes that this gift was something extra (*sed haec erat velut accessio*)—an addition—in order that Christ might show his power in them by some visible gift (*dono isibili*), but he dismisses his own interpretation and makes up a fanciful and pious sounding alternative. Here, in effect, what Calvin offers the Protestant readership of his era is an overt, rationalistic truncation of what an intelligent writer is trying to express within the literary conventions of his day. In my opinion, as a student of Calvin, his cessationistic claims of erasure and truncation, applied without interpretive reservation to New Testament documents, are little more than handwaving excesses par excellence. They are excesses that, even though serving a political, pastoral, and ecclesiastical purpose at the time, may perhaps be nearly unsurpassed in the literary category of interpretive blunders and mistakes. However, in fairness, Calvin's performance in this regard was not motivated solely by literary concerns, but by political ones, and by polemical debate about the miraculous.

In any case, unbeknownst to most participants in the twentieth-century Pentecostal/Charismatic Revival, there is to be detected in this Renewal what is essentially a reappropriation of an ancient interpretive Greco-Roman approach that values and appreciates context, literary coherence,

7. *Commentariorum Joannis Calvini*, 30.

cohesion, repetition and variation, and the intention of an intelligent author, serving to bring First Corinthians 11:5a back into the context of Paul's thought. In addition, the literary emphasis underpinning first-century rhetorical culture on exemplarity and precedent in narrative composition is also newly grasped, in my opinion, through the hidden assistance of the Holy Spirit.

The renewal of this commonsensical approach is interested in interpretation, not in proof-texting, and wants to find out what Paul actually thinks. Of course proof-texting is far from eliminated at this stage, but entrenched dedication to it among laypersons is overcome. There arises sufficient discontent with repeating and abusing fragmentary excerpts from the past. Unarticulated presuppositions that hide the text from later readers are intrinsically discarded. Global Pentecostalism is born. World evangelism receives a pneumatological assist.

A personal Pentecost, according to the examples and precedents of that phenomenon set out by Luke's two-volume narrative to Theophilus, is considered to be available for every disciple-believer-witness who prays for it. The meaning of Spirit-giftedness and Spirit-reception expressed by Paul in First Corinthians 1:4–8; 2:12–14, thoughts no doubt framed out of his personal experience and reflection upon the significance of that experience, receives some possible interpretive light and connection to First Corinthians 12–14. New Testament worship is renewed; there is clapping of hands, joyful noise, dancing in the Spirit, prayer and supplication, tarrying, trembling, and astonishment. The Bible is recaptured as a grand narrative in which the people of God have a part and can fully fit. The people of God are allies with New Testament characters. The people of God are coparticipants with New Testament characters. There is new, thoughtful, and experiential recognition that the heavenly Jesus and the earthly Jesus are somehow one and that the Holy Spirit unites them. *Former ecclesiastical, ideological, and political concerns supposedly validated by proof-texting are pushed into the background.* They are pushed out and a different method of thinking and of establishing belief, one less philosophically inclined, a more accurate, scripturally based belief system in the view of many, takes their place. This pleases the Holy Spirit. The anointing of the Holy Spirit is recognized and given due respect.

To continue with this example from the New Testament that illustrates the new approach—a currently dominant interpretive practice, although with some notable exceptions that still cling to proof-texting—I must mention again, dear Theo, what I have already shared in our pastoral conversations. I speak again of the procedure of *reading front to back*. A New Testament document, as any other piece of competently written literature, must be read front to back. This is how an author intends his or her work to be read, thoughtfully front to back. When something is not clear, then one rereads. One might then, in this case, reread back to front and then again front to back. The author is respected for a desire to produce clarity and accordingly his or her work is read front to back. Just saying how great the Bible is and saying how much one believes in the Bible and then proof-texting an author to make him fit past dogma is inconsistent. This performance makes no literary sense and is disconnected from the Greco-Roman rhetorical culture in which the New Testament documents were written. Global Pentecostalism and the international Charismatic Renewal reject this performance as fundamentally flawed. It is no longer acceptable to imply that a New Testament writer's thought can possibly be known by proof-texting. Instead, one must read contextually front to back, as any competent writer would expect a letter or a narrative to be read.

Reading Paul's first letter to "the church of God which is at Corinth" (1 Cor 1:2) front to back, from First Corinthians

11:5a one comes across First Corinthians 14:34–35. The immediately preceding context (14:1, 3, 24–25, 29–33) shows that Paul is giving guidelines about how the content of prophecies should be judged or discerned and about a workable procedure regulating individuals who offer prophetic ministry. His guidance is that all may prophesy so that all may learn and be encouraged. Keeping silent is part of the collective process (14:30b). Further, the "spirits of prophets are subject to prophets" (14:32). This brings us to First Corinthians 14:34-35, "Let the women be silent in the churches, for it is not permitted for them to speak, but let them be in submission, as the law also says (v.34). If they wish to inquire about something, let them question their own husbands at home (v.35)."

In the proof-texting tradition verse 35 is quickly ignored. Verse 35 is not useful, although it sheds a good deal of light in this context on verse 34. The tradition of modern cessationism only wants to see and hear verse 34. Verse 35 is disconnected from verse 34 and sent into eclipse, given that it suggests that the motivation for these women speaking out and raising questions was a desire to learn, perhaps interrupting people who were trying to prophesy or perhaps questioning them and trying to clarify or resolve a timely issue. Perhaps women and men who had valid prophecies to be judged were being marginalized because some women raised too many questions during discussions about discernment. While the entire context can never be entirely clear to us, there is enough clarity to suggest there was something about situations of this nature that was engendering questions and debate. Rather than modestly trying to understand the circumstances, the interpretive style of some simply extracts verse thirty-four and applies it to all cultures and all times. As an extracted fragment it no longer represents Paul's contextual thinking. However, it is employed in pamphlets in some "Bible-belt" zones and as a revered snippet it is repeated over and over. Gradually, it generates a belief system that accommodates the insular, male-dominated, cultural norms of some. Instead of changing these, it adapts Christianity to them, although that is not what happened in early Christianity. Verse thirty-four alone is "sound doctrine." It becomes the "word of God." Let's ask why?

Politically, I suspect that we can see why. The proof-texting tradition today might be viewed as seeking to preserve the Evangelical Protestant concerns of some, along with ecclesiastical male power and a belief system that supports and maintains these concerns. When challenged, this belief system may become highly reactive, but perhaps not considerate of alternative views or the reasons for them. Perhaps this protectionism is a part of human weakness. In any case, allowing thoughts into the churches that could challenge established and settled beliefs, beliefs that over time have become absolute, is naturally considered dangerous. (However, dear Theo, although missionaries trained in the new approach may be cast out, they have kept preaching anyway.[8] Perhaps a spirituality that keeps passion for the kingdom in the forefront is a worthy mission for being cast out.) Politically, it possibly may seem better for some to keep saying how great the Bible is, while at the same time being less than forthcoming about how narrowly selected passages excised from it supposedly support controversial

8. For example, Luce, "Paul's Missionary Methods" and "Great Physician"; Hyatt, "Spirit-Filled Women"; Kimberly Alexander, "Ministry of Healing"; Estrelda Alexander, *Women of Azusa, passim*; and Butler, *Women in the Church of God in Christ, passim*. The preaching cited here is by individuals who were cast out by some both because of their gender and their message of the "Five-Fold Gospel." This gospel highlights Jesus as savior, sanctifier, baptizer in the Holy Spirit, healer, and soon coming king (cf. Land "Pentecostal Spirituality as Vision").

claims about subjects upon which New Testament writers themselves—if allowed to speak for themselves—may actually shed a good deal of light.

I have encountered the following honest attitudes among scholars whose incomes and families might potentially be jeopardized by a too free-ranging discussion: explaining things to the faithful could be risky; it may be better to just occasionally mention what has always been ignored; we like ourselves the way we are; the Holy Spirit, even if recognizable, is too vague a notion to possibly motivate any substantial change in an ingrained belief system; a post "apostolic-age" Holy Spirit is not in practicality as relevant today as the Holy Spirit must have been in the "apostolic age"; would we even miss the Holy Spirit if he decided to go elsewhere?; our doctrines must be in charge here and we do believe in biblical interpretation, but if established results within our faith tradition are challenged, we will most likely have to devote our attention to interpretation elsewhere; how could centuries of tradition be wrong?; and, how can we admit mistakes? Of course, good scholars always respect the research and insights of other working scholars and do not instinctively applaud dogmatism. They must, however, often be prudent and avoid an encounter with strident assertions of ideological inappropriateness and questionable orthodoxy. These fine scholars have little ecclesiastical or administrative leadership to pursue the key questions: "How do we know?" and "Why do we believe?"

Getting back to the text, if we keep First Corinthians 11:5a in mind, then the last part of First Corinthians 14:35, verse 35b, "For it is improper for a woman to speak in church," suggests that Paul means here that unless women keep their heads covered—as he has previously said they should do when prophesying—they should not speak in church. Also, 35b is obviously tied in Paul's thought to verse 35a, which takes us back to verse 34. This suggests

Paul is aware that in Corinth there are some women who are interrupting proper ministry by asking questions. These women, Paul writes, should be silent in this regard and ask their husbands at home. Paul is writing from Ephesus, across the Aegean Sea (1 Cor 16:8), but by inspiration and diligent oversight he wants to be firm: these particular women must be silent if they cause a disturbance with their questions. Asking questions is not a proper church ministry. The home is the proper setting for these questions and their own husbands are the proper people to address these questions. Obviously, all women may speak in the churches in their ministry of prophecy and should be accorded the respect that is given to those whom God would use in prophetic ministry—*which may include instruction or teaching so that people may learn* (1 Cor 14:31)—but when it comes to asking questions that apparently are causing confusion (14:33), these questions must be addressed at home by their own husbands.

One has to wonder about what subject these particular women in this particular congregation were so intense with their questions. I have a guess. We have found that in Corinth there were many temples of various Roman religions involving a number of gods. This is typical of major, first-century Roman cities. In some of these temples in Corinth—but most certainly not in all—it may be the case that the worshippers wore a traditional headcovering, perhaps to show respect to the gods, but such a motive is uncertain. I suspect that some Christian women at Corinth were not happy about having to wear headcoverings like some other non-Christian religious women in the city and that this topic was the subject of many intense questions. *Perhaps they wondered, if male circumcision was now believed to be unnecessary as required in Judaism, what was the continued spiritual attraction for female headcoverings?* Perhaps Paul's explanation (1 Cor 11:6–13) or some other explanation appeared elusive. While Paul might not have related the rejection of male circumcision to the rejection of female headcoverings, others may have detected a bothersome inconsistency. Also, while at the Jewish synagogue in the city men would wear headcoverings (some Jewish synagogues in Asia Minor having women as their synagogue leaders), these Christian women in Corinth were not Jews and would see little value in imitating Jewish men (or women) or being like women in some temples devoted to various gods. They wanted to eliminate these traditions, to take the brakes off, but, perhaps, some of the men liked things to be otherwise. Accordingly, this would be a topic of hot discussion and so it is my guess that this quite possibly could be one source of some of their questions.

So, when First Corinthians 11:5a, stating in effect that women who pray or prophesy with an uncovered head are somehow culturally disrespecting their gender, is kept in mind, then First Corinthians 14:34–35 becomes more understandable to those who attempt to grasp Paul's interconnected thinking. A connected thread of coherent thought begins to emerge. There is context that yields more understanding. In any case, there is no need to affirm centuries-old teachings and dogmatic convictions about the cessation of women's ministries based on what Paul writes here. Keeping Paul's belief in women's ministry in mind and keeping in mind that *all*—in Greek the "all" is gender neutral—may prophesy (14:31) and that all should desire to prophesy (14:1), Paul's view of the home as a place to quietly address and discuss questions is quite understandable. Paul believes in the home and that a husband is the head of the house; just as Paul does not believe in dictatorship or undue authority, he does believe in questions and discussion. Women in Christian homes should be submissive and listen to their husbands, but this does not mean that husbands should not listen to their wives. Wives can be right too. Pentecostal preachers often call attention to God telling Abraham to listen to his wife (Gen 21:9–13).

In today's world women may serve as leaders of countries; Finland, Germany, Israel, Norway, the Philippines, and the United Kingdom come to mind. In the U.S. we have distinguished Supreme Court justices, senators, and congresswomen. The current president of the University of Michigan is a woman. Women are awarded Nobel Prizes and serve in every profession, including the divine calling of Christian ministries according to Ephesians 4:11–13, where the heavenly Jesus is rightly taken as a gender-neutral administrator of ministerial emplacement and vocation. To read Ephesians 4:11–13 through the culturally tinged glasses of an earthly, sexual bias does a grave injustice to Paul and his communicative intentions. To do so completely overlooks the mysterious spiritual unity that exists and transcends all cultural boundaries and norms among those who, having believed, are sealed with the Holy Spirit of promise and who can experience the wisdom, revelation, and hope of Christ's calling and heavenly direction (as suggested by Eph 1:13–20). I think the English translation, "And his gifts were that some should be apostles, some prophets, some evangelists, some pastors and teachers, to equip the saints for the work of ministry, for building up the body of Christ" (Eph 4:11–12, RSV),[9] captures Paul's original intent and would be difficult to improve upon. The Ephesians surely expected the heavenly Jesus to be placing these ministries into their congregation(s) and to support them. The heavenly directed sealing with the Holy Spirit of promise of those who have believed (Eph 1:13) is probably a communally accepted way of identifying an experientially recognized validation of their individual ministerial calling,

9. All translations in this present study are my own unless otherwise noted.

a valid credentialling from the heavenly Jesus. The experience of sealing and the Spirit-language associated with it that is used here show a possible literary link to the Spirit-language employed later in Luke-Acts where examples and precedents of Spirit-reception afford readers a narrative-rhetorical clarification of the particular expression found in the earlier Ephesian letter.

In any case, those who are called to equip the saints for the work of the ministry might expect to serve effectively in a gender-neutral manner within various capacities according to the purpose and plan of the heavenly Jesus. After all, there was much missionary and evangelistic work to be done in Asia, which remains true yet today. Also, in the ancient Hebrew Scriptures, women functioned in leadership and spiritual roles, suggesting an expectation for women's ministries in the new covenant in continuity with New Testament documents. (Miriam and Hulda served as prophetesses who had significant participation in God's purpose [Exod 15:20–21; 2 Kgs 22:14–20]. Deborah, a "mother in Israel," was a prophetess and served as a judge of Israel, combining spiritual, military, and judicial leadership in times of conflict [Judg 4–5]. The prophetess Anna [Luke 2:36–38] who spoke of Jesus and redemption probably somehow served in continuity with this prophetic tradition.)

None of these aforementioned prophetesses can possibly be viewed as exerting some kind of strange, sexist "authority" over men. The texts describing their ministries do not suggest that they were viewed askance or regarded as unusual. Similarly and with new spiritual force, Paul's thought about the effect of the contemporary ministry of the heavenly Lord Jesus Christ—a ministry that he undoubtedly finds consistent with what he knows about the ministry of the earthly Jesus—is that racial, social, and sexual barriers have been broken down so that all those "in Christ" are made one (Gal 3:28). Christians in Galatia who had received the promise of the Spirit through faith (Gal 3:14b) must realize that now there is neither male nor female in the new spiritual community. The exclusionary features of their secular culture did not carry over to heavenly governance of those made one in Christ Jesus. Spirit-reception through faith, and its effects (Gal 3:2, 5), should motivate such an experiential understanding of what Christianity really is, according to Paul.

In my view, what he is expressing in Galatians 3:28, as a result of Spirit-reception and ensuing reflection, is that secular cultural norms and mandates are not at all to be considered as imitations of the genuine heavenly intention. There is a new, radical, and spiritually creative pattern to be followed. Male domination is a paltry aberration of what heaven intends for those in Christ. In Christ's redeemed kingdom there is no domination or subjugation of anyone by anybody as in earthly cultures afflicted by human sinfulness. This much seems clear, but since Paul's Spirit-reception language here in Galatians is not clarified by exemplarity, it is difficult, if nearly impossible, for later readers to obtain certainty about what Paul intends to communicate about the role of the Holy Spirit and about the personal reception of the Spirit. Paul does imply, however, that the Holy Spirit, whom the Galatians have received through faith (Gal 3:2, 5), will substantiate and help them understand what he is saying.

There is a body of persuasive evidence to suggest that Luke, who, writing some time later in an interconnected communicative Christian network, sought out and read a copy of Paul's letter to the Galatians and that he then duly clarifies and improves upon Paul's discourse at this juncture with the proper and expected narrative-rhetorical examples and precedents of Spirit-reception that serve to stimulate fresh rereadings of Galatians. This reasonable and rhetorically attractive suggestion concerning Luke's employment of Paul's Spirit-language falls short of a formal proof, but Luke makes it clear, for example, in presenting Peter's programmatic speech in Acts 2 (see Acts 2:17–18) wherein both sons and daughters will be blessed and highly favored with the gift of the Holy Spirit, in concert with Paul's perception, that now there is neither male nor female. *All* will be equipped for ministry according to God's sovereign agenda and should therefore duly seek to be so equipped. Nonetheless, while women are equal in the Spirit in ministry to men, hence Paul's contextual language of there no longer being male or female, the final governance in the Christian home, after discussion and *mutual submission*, is the husband. This model of home life is important to Paul. Here, the husband is the head of the wife (Eph 5:23)—in an atmosphere of mutual submission (Eph 5:21)—so as to place greater responsibility on the husband for caring for his wife. He is to give himself for her in love as Christ gave himself for the Church. *Both in the home and in the church mutual submission is the controlling principle.*

3

First Timothy and Its Context

ERE IN First Timothy is the flagship fragment of the Evangelical Protestant polemic against women's ministries. This fragment may, unfortunately, be used without mercy and without compassion to humiliate, embarrass, discourage, and intimidate women who are being called into various ministries by our Lord. While perhaps especially intense in "Bible-belt" zones, such attitudes are not confined geographically to any one country. Spirit-filled women (in the sense of Luke's interior metaphor of filling at Acts 2:4, probably adopted from previous Christian tradition) who would move on beyond Pentecost to "regions beyond"—as those portrayed in Acts 1:8, 14 would have in some sense eventually wanted to do—may actually be harassed in "Bible-belt" interpretive zones and told that their evangelistic intentions are not "biblical," supposedly based on this passage extracted from Paul's correspondence with pastor Timothy and other proof-texted passages. Timothy had a Greek father and a Jewish mother who was a believer (Acts 16:1). The fact that Paul's first letter to Timothy was written (probably from Rome) and hand-carried to this young pastor in Ephesus (1 Tim 1:3), a great Roman seaport city in Asia well known for its religious practices, is usually not brought into the popularized interpretation of some. No consideration or reflection of the Roman world bearing upon what probably occasioned the communication, with respect to some women that Timothy was facing in Ephesus, normally comes into the conversation among those who may have uncritically fallen under the influence of the modern cessationist mindset.

When I use the concept of "modern cessationist mindset" I am struggling with trying to identify how this worldview affects interpretation. As I am able to grasp it, not being a professional anthropologist, this is a mindset that has posited that God will not engage in a number of spiritual activities since he is presumed to have invoked their cessation after the New Testament was finished and the last ink had dried on the last papyrus sheet. The social attitudes toward women prevalent in the fifteenth and sixteenth centuries and the political adoption by the Reformers of an "apostolic-age" style of interpretation against the miraculous were intertwined and became concretized into a Christian ideology that has been promoted and embellished within the history of Protestantism. This led to a belief system that sought for biblical confirmation. Its imposition upon the New Testament writers, or to put it another way, reading these Christian thinkers through that ideological lens, seems to have been an unavoidable outcome for some that has affected interpretation in peculiar ways.

Peter's speech in Acts 2 and his projection of Joel's prophecy at Acts 2:17–18 about dreams, visions, and inspired prophetic speech by men *and* women beyond narrative time is one New Testament excerpt which must bear the weight of this theory. This inspired prophetic ministry of men and women appears to extend, in this immediate context, until the day of the Lord. However, what an individual New Testament writer's authorial intention is or is not may not really enter into interpretation at all if an absolute theory of cessationism is imposed upon that writer from the outset. This is what I mean by reading through an ideological lens. What appears to have become central in the scheme of a modern cessationistic mindset is a determination to embrace a set of past Christian cultural norms that are now supposedly validated by the Bible. (Is this different from Roman Catholicism that by contrast openly appeals to church tradition, as well as to scripture, as a source of truth?) In this mindset the supposed "sufficiency of scripture"—like the sufficiency of the Torah in Judaism—is touted as a main public argument for believing whatever the latest edition of accommodating study Bibles has to say, always failing to mention that in New Testament Christianity Christ's presence is mediated by the Holy Spirit. This tactic also often distorts what scripture actually says about itself and forgets to mention that scripture is "sufficient" only if it is interpreted according to proof-texting methods that confirm certain teachings and dogmatic convictions, which have gradually concretized, particularly in the past two centuries of Evangelical Protestantism, into a discursively and narratively disruptive scheme of interpretation. It is via this sort of contextually extracted detachment and deployment of this flagship fragment from First Timothy, dear Theo, where the original meaning and authorial intent it represents are insufficiently sought, that you will encounter what I am characterizing as a modern cessationistic mindset. Obviously, if women must be silent then they cannot prophesy, which seems to be the endgame.

It is also difficult to detect in this approach any consideration or reflection aimed at trying to square an understanding of this passage with Luke's later overview in Acts or with the earlier First Corinthians, even though Paul wrote First Corinthians from Ephesus. This is unsurprising, since some Evangelical Protestants have long asserted that Luke's second volume is merely a work of history, not a teaching book, and therefore cannot be used to establish doctrine. However, when the identical language used in Acts to exemplify and personify activities of the Holy Spirit is found in the earlier letters of Paul, perhaps suggesting that Luke desires to initiate and stimulate a fresh reading of Paul and extend Paul's proper influence via an imitative literary method,[1] such an interpretive dictum is essentially at odds with the theology and pneumatology of the early Christians. It is surely correct that "The resurrection of Jesus and their experience of the Spirit confirm for them that the message of Jesus is true and that he is now confirmed by God as Messiah and Lord. He is therefore now active from heaven through a variety of agencies."[2]

Instead of driving a wedge between the pneumatology of Paul and the Lukan characters, including Paul, more thought needs to be given to Paul's probable conceptual and linguistic connection with the Jerusalem-Petrine tradition of earliest Christianity that is clearly reflected in Paul's own appeal to previous Christian tradition. This linguistic connection is also reflected, for example, in the ministry of Peter and John at Acts 8:15, 17 and of Ananias at Acts 9:17. According to this narrative, Peter and John's Spirit-reception language and Ananias' Spirit-filling language is established in Christian descriptive practice through identification with experience before Paul's conversion. Similarly, with respect to First Timothy, more thought needs to be given to using Paul's thought from First Corinthians properly with respect to women's ministry and to taking into account Luke-Acts in that regard because of its attention to Jerusalem-Petrine beginnings and to the historical Paul. Perhaps more thought

1. Brodie, "Towards," 116, notes "Luke's general practice of setting out a positive vivid ideal" to the end that "there are two possible explanations for the data: either an extraordinary series of coincidences or, more, simply, that Luke the *littérateur* used a literary method." Elbert, "Possible Literary Links," suggests the latter with respect to Luke's employment of Paul's earlier Spirit-reception and Spirit-giftedness language, experientially expressive language probably in widespread use.

2. Marshall, *New Testament Theology*, 205.

might be afforded here to other New Testament documents if that would help shed light on Paul's intended meaning as he tries to help Timothy with a pastoral problem.

Instead of this interdocumentary approach, in the public sphere, what is repeated over and over by the mindset I am attempting to counteract is just the reverse assertion—an astonishing claim misguidedly touted as "scriptural"—that First Timothy 2:11–12 defines Paul's inspired and godly view about the role of all women at all times and at all places. This claim, in my view, is false, as well as pastorally harmful.

Fragmentation and extraction and isolation of Paul's thought here—supposed thought that is uncritically employed to fit theoretical schemes of traditionally invented extrabiblical epochs that appear to constrain and confine God—may reign supreme among some in "Bible-belt" zones. Now, to preserve what is right is admirable; to stubbornly attempt to preserve what is seriously questionable without vigorous investigation, consideration, or reflection is less than admirable. With all due respect, we should try to stimulate a real desire for genuine interpretation. Objective truth exists within biblical texts and an element of exploration is necessary along with the preservation of sound doctrine. One thing seems, to me, very clear: First Timothy 2:11–12 cannot be proof-texted and excised out of the entire New Testament context, including the context in First Timothy, and then turned into an authoritarian absolute that appears to distort and deny the distinctively new Christian cultural, missionary, and social context forged within the New Testament world. This includes the potential misreading of the entirety of Paul's thought with respect to women's ministries within the Christianity of his day as reflected in all of his letters. In my opinion, if Christianity goes down this road, it does so against the grain of some significant New Testament thought and will find it difficult to convince the majority within the disciplines of biblical interpretation and New Testament scholarship.

In spite of this somewhat tense atmosphere for the ongoing task of biblical interpretation that such an ecclesiastical appropriation of First Timothy 2:11–12 creates, there are many commonsensical folk who are not totally indoctrinated by premature claims fashioned around an "apostolic-age" style of proof-texting. For example, in the genre of study Bibles, the *Dake Annotated Reference Bible* (first self-published in 1963, Atlanta, Georgia), attempts to shed an alternative light on the First Timothy passage. Dake, to his credit, appears to realize that 2:11–12, if proof-texted, would contradict or conflict with what Paul and other New Testament writers have to say elsewhere on this subject, so he posits some reasonable ideas but is still overly influenced by Evangelical Protestant culture to keep legitimate women's ministries under the authority of men. However, dear Theo, I want to move beyond popular comments if I may and give you a look at the Roman world of women in Ephesus, because such a look can make this passage come to life and make it understandable in its original context. Here, the relevant social and political context in Ephesus pertaining to women, a historical context that would have been very real to both Paul and Timothy, must be taken into account in understanding this passage. They would both, I believe, recognize the leading and guiding and the anointing of the Holy Spirit as they contemplated the pastoral problem they were facing. We are allied with them in this regard, and we can understand and participate in the recognizable activity and leading of the Holy Spirit today throughout the world, just as in the first century. The Holy Spirit eventually trumps bad dogma and he is very patient.

Paul mentions the home seven times in his first letter to Timothy, along with child bearing, which then took place in the home. *The home, and what originates therein, supplies much of the context for First Timothy.* It seems clear, when Paul writes to Timothy that women are to "remain quiet" (1 Tim 2:12b), he obviously *cannot* be thinking about the role of a woman in prophetic ministry as in Acts and First Corinthians, or in the role of copastoring, or in the role of a deaconess, or in the ministry of a female apostle such as Junia (the chapter on "Romans and Related Observations" of this present study takes a careful look at these latter ministries). Here, in First Timothy, Paul must have some other situation in mind because one cannot "remain quiet" in these ministries. Along with other scholars cited in the bibliography, my belief is that what Paul has in mind here are situations in home life where a wife receives instructions from her own husband, something she should do quietly and with submissiveness (1 Tim 2:11). Paul offers his reason as to why this attitude is appropriate (1 Tim 2:13–15). However, again, this does not mean that Paul is against discussion and questions.

The immediately preceding context to First Timothy 2:11–12 treats how Christian women should dress, so there was probably a discussion about this topic that Timothy had to confront because women had questions about it, perhaps like the issue of headcoverings in the Corinthian congregation. In the situation here in Ephesus, which evidently had become a controversial issue of involved discussion, a woman is not to exercise authority over a man. The "man" here is most probably a woman's own husband and the setting is surely at home. The man takes the lead in teaching about the contextual problem (1 Tim 2:9) when discussion of it becomes appropriate at home, where these women should listen and be submissive, not to be instructing their husbands as to how well, in their opinion, their socially appropriate and socially conforming dressing habits meet the standard of Christian attire. Paul employs a word here, a word found *only* at this place in the New Testament, probably because these women were so intense on this issue that they were taking authority over their husbands. The Greek verb is *authentein* (1 Tim 2:12), meaning to have authority, to domineer. It is related to the noun *authentēs*, meaning master. This usage reflects a situation that Paul wishes to correct.

When Paul says here (2:12) that he does not allow (*ouk epitrepō*, I do not permit) a woman to teach, he is thinking about the women who need to learn from their husbands at home. Employing the immediate context, which is identically harmonious with what we know about the religious context in first-century Ephesus, Paul is correcting religious women of high social status who actually had fine clothes and jewels to wear and could come to worship with highly coiffured hair. These women had the money to shop for expensive gowns and handcrafted jewelry and to employ hairdressers. The Greek verb Paul uses here (I allow or permit, *epitrepō*) is common enough, but it is interesting that there are a number of instances of its usage—as in 2:12—where it cannot be taken to mean, "I am permanently banning 'something or other.'" While there are a few exceptions, this is, nevertheless, a verb that commonly implies a prohibition for a specific period of time in a specific case. This common usage, which a Greek speaker would be aware of, makes a good deal of sense in the context of this entire letter to Timothy. We have already seen how Paul encourages women to prophesy and that prophesying can include teaching and instruction. Here, Paul is correcting a specific culturally sensitive problem. He could have written, "I will never permit a woman to teach" (something that would be inconsistent with how the real Paul regards women's ministries alongside his own), but he did not do so. The textual implication here, one consistent with the underlying cultural situation, is that when the problem is corrected and these women have learned enough to be able to teach properly, they might be called into the ministry just like anyone else.[3]

Paul does not use the word or concept *authentein* (1 Tim 2:12) anywhere else, a verbal idea implying authority with potentially domineering overtones, nor any concept remotely like it, to discuss preaching or prophesying or teaching by women *or* by men. In these Christian activities, one certainly does *not* exert this kind of authority or project such an attitude toward one's hearers. Such a rather ambitious assertion by some Evangelical Protestants, claiming that women cannot fulfill their Spirit-called ministries because they might manifest an attitude of *authentein* and *authentēs*, may be over the top. Perhaps it might be somewhat unwise to so incautiously subject Christian women in general to such a strained sexist insinuation, that their ministry might exercise demeaning authority if men are exposed to it. Paul makes no such statement. This attitude is against the probable thought of the real Paul—who is not writing here about the improper prophetic ministry of women. Instead the issue here is one of Ephesian women under the influence of very strong social and cultural norms not being able to grasp new Christian ideas about modest apparel and life in a proper Christian home. Obviously, Paul does not think that all Christian women in Ephesus have this problem. In extending greetings from Claudia and all the brethren in Rome to Timothy in Ephesus (2 Tim 4:21b), he also extends his cordial greetings to Prisca and Aquila (2 Tim 4:19). We recall that this pastoral team, husband and wife (Acts 18:2), were serving a church in their house in Ephesus (1 Cor 16:8, 19) at the time. There was evidently more than one house church in Ephesus, probably established during

3. So too, Marshall, *New Testament Theology*, 402, who observes that "The restriction here on women teaching was necessary because of specific circumstances and is not a timeless principle."

Paul's two years of daily lecturing and evangelistic supervision at the school of Tyrannus (Acts 19:9–10).

Perhaps it may be apropos to mention that within global Pentecostalism and the international Charismatic Renewal today, and rightly so, at least in my reading of New Testament texts, it is *servanthood*, rather than some kind of presumed authority or mastery, that is the focal point of the Spirit-led ministry for both men and women. *In the ministry of evangelistic servanthood, the recognizable and respected anointing of the Spirit of Jesus continues to validate both the messenger and the message when ministers go to "regions beyond" (2 Cor 10:16), whether they be men or women, Brazilian, Chinese, Nepalese, or Nigerian.*

Why then would some Christian women in Ephesus be so influenced to dress in the way Paul describes? Once that is understood, then Paul's statements become far more understandable. Most Christian women were not wealthy and could not afford to spend their spare money, if indeed they had any, from their husbands' incomes on lavish clothes, ornate jewelry, and the expense of hairdressers (1 Tim 2:9). Even if some women had extra money, why would they be prone to spend it in such an ostentatious manner in order for their appearance to garner so much attention? The answer is found in the Roman religious life in Ephesus.

In Roman cities there were many religious sects and temples, all of which had active political connections with Roman rule and society. In Ephesus there was a temple to a feminine god named Artemis. That was her Greek name. Her Roman name was Diana. She is mentioned in Acts 19:23–28, 34–37, and there you can get a glimpse of her cultural influence. There was a sympathetic bond between the goddess and her devotees. She was Ephesus' divine patron and the claim by Demetrius that Artemis was worshipped throughout the world (Acts 19:27) was certainly not mere hyperbole. A second-century inscription detailing the civic importance of appropriate feasts and festivals notes that "Since the goddess Artemis, leader of our city, is honored not only in her own homeland, which she has made the most illustrious of all cities through her own divine nature, but also among Greeks and barbarians, the result is that everywhere her shrines and sanctuaries have been established, and temples have been founded for her and altars dedicated to her because of the visible manifestations effected by her."[4]

Through archaeology and research into Roman civilization, we have learned a good deal about this goddess and about another prominent feminine goddess named Isis. The appealing Hellenistic cult of Isis was widely spread by wandering groups throughout the Greco-Roman world. With religious roots in Egyptian culture, her veneration spread throughout the Roman Empire. Both Artemis/Diana and Isis had temples in all major Roman cities. Ephesus was especially prominent in this regard. Temples there were served by priestesses of the goddess Artemis/Diana. Priestesses also facilitated worship of the goddess Isis. Initiation rites accentuated the absolute power of these female deities. Arousing pageantry led to a strong sense of connectedness among initiates. These temple activities had deep social, cultural, financial, and political roots in Roman cities, particularly in Ephesus. The priestesses exerted considerable public influence. They had an accepted social status. They would be imitated. Children could be named after them. It would be fashionable to look like them. They kept men in their place, probably with domineering authority compatible with their religious and civil status, when men came to worship in the temples. They took care of the sacred symbols of worship and of the sacred texts describing these deities. They man-

---

4. Horsley, "Artemis," 154.

aged ceremonies open to the public. That was their role as priestesses of Artemis/Diana and of Isis.

When we study the temple statues, engravings, paintings, and stone carvings of these goddesses and their priestesses, we find exactly what Paul is speaking about in First Timothy 2:9. Their dress was ostentatious when compared with how most women dressed. The archeological evidence shows clearly that their hair was carefully braided and coiffured by hairdressers, and they wore highly ornamental jewelry. Women from this setting had been converted to Christianity, and they brought these socially acceptable excesses with them. Although normal for them, these excesses did not set a good example for the poor. Before they were converted, husbands of women who imitated the socially prominent priestesses naturally went along with these appearances, as did the rest of Ephesian society.

Now, in this religious atmosphere, their husbands and pastor Timothy had the responsibility to change such women's attitudes, but more than likely they continued to encounter a worldly resistance to change—hence the instruction for these women to "remain quiet," something that such women would find difficult to do on this issue. After Timothy's ministry and after Paul's earlier ministry in Ephesus and Asia for two years at Tyrannus' school, this social influence and imitative behavior was obviously still a problem. The cultural ethos of Ephesus, a Roman city in the eastern half of the empire with distinctive and influential religious traditions, did not readily accommodate itself overnight to the sudden claims of an unknown tentmaker from Tarsus. The richness of the local heritage of divinity with its festival to the goddess Artemis and celebrations of her birth, coupled with culturally related political and economic interests, complicated the missionary endeavor.

Paul's language at First Timothy 2:11–12 fits very reasonably with this scenario and Paul's contextual remarks—again reading Paul's letter front to back—would be easily understandable to Timothy in the life setting we can confidently place him in through research into Roman history. That is how this letter in its temporal context is best interpreted. This reasonable interpretation is also entirely consistent and harmonious with the real Paul we encounter elsewhere. This consistency and harmoniousness is important if we take the Bible to be a grand narrative, one that is cohesive and coherent.

When we read on to the qualifications for deacons, we also see that "Women must likewise be dignified . . ." (1 Tim 3:11), which probably refers equally, in this context of husbands and wives (1 Tim 3:2, 12), to women who are either deacons' wives or to deaconesses or to prospective deaconesses. As we will see in Paul's earlier letter to the Romans, he is appreciative of the ministry of deaconesses.

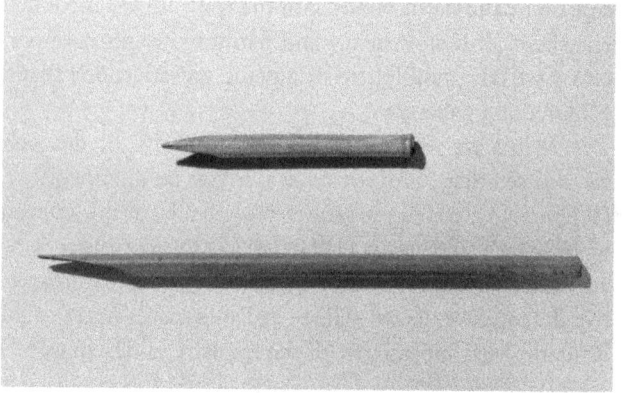

Roman Reed Pens

4

Luke's Second Volume
and a Personal Testimony

WHEN ONE looks at Paul as personified in Luke's second book dedicated to Theophilus (Luke 1:3; Acts
1:1)—a book by an anonymous and rhetorically skillful
writer that many believe to be Luke, the beloved physician
(Col 4:14)—and when one also looks at what Paul writes
in his letter to the Romans, one finds, not unexpectedly,
a strong harmoniousness with our understanding of Paul
from First Corinthians wherein he expresses appreciation
for the role of women in prophesying (1 Cor 11:5a; 14:1,
39). Since the letter to Rome was written from Corinth
(Rom 16:23; 1 Cor 1:14; Acts 18:7), we could expect an
empathetic connection in Paul's appreciation for women
who are ministering in Rome with those who are prophesying in Corinth. Details of this solid empathetic connection
are what we find, as I will explore in the chapter on "Romans
and Related Observations" of this present study. Here, in
this chapter, I would draw attention to Luke's portrayal and
personification of Peter, Paul, and Apollos with respect to
this apparent collaborative connection in what we call "The
Book of Acts," although I suspect that Luke, had he named
his second volume himself, would have called it something
like "The Gospel of the Holy Spirit."

Luke, an educated Greek-speaking and literary-minded Christian, obviously thinks, based on what he actually

writes, that women in his day will prophesy. He gives no hint that this inspired and revelatory giftedness will be restricted to his original readership or that it ceased before his double work was completed. He imposes no temporal chasm between his characters and his original readers or between them and all later readers. Luke believed that Peter, a significant figure, had also been of this frame of mind as well. Luke records that on the day of Pentecost, a group of disciple-believer-witnesses, evidently all participants in the events of the Third Gospel in one way or another, were assembled in Jerusalem. The one hundred and twenty men and women, including Mary the mother of Jesus and his brothers, are awaiting in prayer the promised gift of the Holy Spirit. After that prophetic experience, in this case entailing inspired speech about the mighty deeds of God in various tongues unknown to these believers,[1] Peter provides an explanation. The first part of Peter's programmatic speech, adopting a quote from the prophet Joel, reads as follows (Acts 2:17–18):

> And it shall be in the last days, says God, I will
> pour out of my Spirit upon all flesh, and your
> sons and your daughters will prophesy, and your

---

1. This first personal Spirit-reception is framed by a connected narrative sequence that concludes with an invitation extended to readers: Luke 3:16; 11:13; 24:49; Acts 1:4–5, 13–15; 2:1–4, 38–39. In this cohesive movement of the story, readers may discern Lukan expectations and a theological motive. Luke provides Theophilus with continuity from the original prophesy of John the Baptist about Jesus' role as baptizer in the Holy Spirit to its first fulfillment from the heavenly Jesus, who now as heavenly Lord and Christ pours the Spirit out (Acts 2:33, 36) upon disciple-believers. It is also interesting to note that Luke pays the same theological attention to the fulfillment of the angel's prophecy that Jesus will be a savior (Luke 2:11), providing examples and precedents of Jesus' earthly and heavenly ministry in that regard (Luke 7:33–50; Acts 16:30–31) that could serve as potential points of application and identification for his readership.

> young men will see visions, and your old men
> will dream dreams. Even upon my servants,
> both men and women, I will pour out my Spirit
> in those days, and they will prophesy.

In the central part of the speech (Acts 2:33), Peter makes clear that it is Jesus, now raised from among the dead and exalted to the right hand of the Father, who has poured forth the promise of the Holy Spirit that is now both seen and heard by observers.

The narrative foreground of this event—disciple-believers receiving the gift of the Holy Spirit—impresses upon all readers the significance of the event, namely that this group of one hundred and twenty people, witnesses to the resurrection (Luke 24:48), have, according to the instructions of the resurrected Jesus himself, received some additional and mysterious spiritual power. This seems to be an interior spiritual enablement tailored to individual recipients, coupled with new communicative ability to praise and worship God in a nonrational and prophetic manner, so as to better equip disciple-believers for whatever ministries the Lord may have in mind for each of them. Aside from providing assurance of Jesus' resurrection and of his heavenly location from where the gift of the Holy Spirit is poured out, as recognized by Peter (Acts 2:23–24, 32–36), how can such an event and its implications be rationally understood? Luke records these foregrounding words of Jesus, which were no doubt well-remembered: "You will receive power when the Holy Spirit comes upon you, and you will be my witnesses both in Jerusalem and in all Judea and Samaria, and unto the remotest part (or extremity) of the earth" (Acts 1:8).

When hearers of this inspired prophetic speech absorb Peter's explanation and ask what to do, Peter urges hearers to repent and to be baptized in Jesus' name for the remission of sins. When those conditions are met, Peter—portrayed here with typical Greco-Roman rhetorical personification that I think Theophilus would find readily understandable—promises them the same gift of the Holy Spirit that he himself has just received, concluding his speech as follows: "Repent, and let each of you be baptized in the name of Jesus for the forgiveness of your sins, and you will receive the gift of the Holy Spirit, for the promise is unto you and your children and to all who afar off, to as many as the Lord our God may call" (Acts 2:38–39).

Now a Christian reader like Theophilus would gain, I suggest, the immediate impression that being so Spirit-filled (Acts 2:4) would be a good thing, since he was apparently one of those afar off, beyond narrative time, that Peter envisions. Accordingly, I think he would read the rest of the story with great interest. In Greco-Roman literary circles, when a respected writer projects an experience beyond narrative time, one that he properly illustrates with examples and precedents—such personal experience that could not be projected for the benefit of active readers of mythological texts—this could be grasped as a potentially significant narrative occurrence. After reading front to back, Theophilus could be motivated to imitate the one hundred and twenty characters here and begin to pray for the gift of the Holy Spirit himself, praying with Lukan expectations. If men and women will prophesy according to the prophet Joel and if a reliable historical figure like Peter has promised—via a connective and cohesive reading beginning with the words of John the Baptist, another reliable figure—that Jesus will baptize in the Holy Spirit, it is not difficult to speculate that Theophilus would readily come away from a comprehensive front-to-back reading of Luke-Acts with a desire to explore expectant prayer for the gift of a heavenly person.

Also, irrespective of the various social attitudes toward women in the Roman world, Theophilus would realize, I suggest, that the Christian women among the one hundred and twenty portrayed here have entered a new spiritual domain instituted by God himself through the prophet Joel and now again through Peter. Now, they are experientially aligned with the fulfillment of the prophetic words "your daughters will prophesy . . . upon my servants, both men and women, I will pour out my Spirit in those days, and they will prophesy." This new spiritual domain of the last days is quite evidently *not* of earthly social or cultural origins. Both men and women who are so filled with the Holy Spirit, via a personal baptism by the heavenly Jesus, enter into a prophethood of believers. This prophethood breaks all social and cultural boundaries and exclusions related to gender. Disciple-believers so equipped can prophesy, preach, teach, exhort, and respond to any divine call that the heavenly Lord Jesus desires for them. This new prophethood is not ordered by earthly secular notions of division based on gender, class, race, education, or politics. While outwardly, this community of prophets could appear to observers to conform to worldly norms and cultural restrictions, there is now a greater unseen world to be appreciated and appropriated in a distinctive Christian unity.

As to Paul, an engagement with the communicative network of Christian communities and missionaries in the culturally distinctive New Testament world would lead to the recognition that prophesying leads right on to preaching and teaching and engaging in missionary work. I doubt that Theophilus would be surprised at various prophetic activities cited in Acts. These are always employed usefully for the story line. For example, at Acts 21:4, disciples in Tyre, Syria, told Paul "through the Spirit" that he should not go to Jerusalem. Luke would be interested in citing the content of those prophecies because it suits his narrative purpose with regard to Paul eventually being taken to Rome.

Further along on this journey, Paul and apparently Luke as well (note the contextual "we") arrive at Caesarea (Acts 21:8), an important Roman maritime city in Samaria. Samaria is a region where Philip had preached earlier and where Peter and John helped minister the reception of the Holy Spirit to baptized believers (Acts 8:5, 12–18). Caesarea, built by Herod the Great and named in honor of Augustus (Luke 2:1), is where the Roman centurion Cornelius, along with his relatives and close friends, received the gift of the Holy Spirit (Acts 10:1, 24, 44–46). Given that Caesarea was a bustling trade center in Samaria, the main Mediterranean port of Palestine, the seat of Roman governance, and a destination of convenient Roman roads, I suspect that Christianity, as portrayed by Luke in Acts 8 involving the ministry of Philip, Peter, and John, had already arrived via such Christian travelers to that city before Peter's ministry to the Roman centurion Cornelius. Barnabus and the brethren had once brought Paul to Caesarea and Luke notes that the church was built up and multiplied in Samaria (Acts 9:30–31). Something had sparked Cornelius' interest. However, apparently Christianity was still confined there to Jews, Samaritans, and those converted to Judaism, since Peter is surprised by God-fearing Gentiles receiving the Spirit, remarking that "Can anyone forbid water for these to be baptized, who received the Holy Spirit as we" (Acts 10:47). Luke's original reader, Theophilus, probably a Gentile himself and perhaps a Roman official, could resonant with the significance of Peter's vision (10:9–17) and this detailed portrayal of Spirit-reception.

Sometime later Paul and Luke stop in Caesarea and stay with Philip the evangelist and his four prophesying daughters for several days (Acts 21:8–9). Philip's daughters evidently impressed Luke as women whose prophetic ministry was worthwhile. Just as before in Tyre (Acts 21:4a), I expect that disciples congregated and were sought out to fellowship with Paul and visit in Philip's house. As far as the story line is concerned, Peter's programmatic speech of Acts 2 has already drawn attention to the forthcoming prophetic ministry of men and women, so mentioning these four daughters "who were prophetesses" (21:9) is useful to the continuity of the story line in that connection. However, it is interesting that Luke does not record the content of probable prophecies that he heard there from Philip's four daughters. I would suggest that the reason for this is that they did not contribute sufficiently to his narrative purpose, similar to the point that although Luke evidently makes use of various elements of Paul's letters, he does not mention that Paul wrote letters. This particular information also does not suit his narrative purpose. Not mentioning that a distinguished writer wrote anything, while even at the same time occasionally imitating some of his phrasing and vocabulary, was a common practice among the Greek medical writers of Luke's day with respect to Hippocrates, the father of medicine. Luke's performance in not mentioning that Paul wrote anything is quite consistent with that scientific tradition as well as with a focused narrative purpose.

Lastly, regarding the prophetic ministry of these four women, who were known to prophesy when disciple-believers gathered in Philip's house or perhaps in other house churches, would Paul tell Philip that women were not to speak in church and that Philip's daughters should be silent? Such a scenario is of course ridiculous. Nevertheless, such ridiculous contradictions often occur when a make-it-fit style of proof-texting requires biblical texts to say what they do not really say. These are the questionable and unexamined features of an interpretive scheme that requires the cessation of unnatural-appearing spiritual enablements together with the cessation of women's ministries. Philip's daughters obviously ministered to Christian men as well as to Christian women when disciple-believers gathered. Incongruities like this between the real Paul and the religious culture of contemporary cessationism must be swept under the rug in order to preserve a false picture of Paul as a person who supposedly does not allow women to speak in the churches. This is inconsistent with a proper understanding both of Paul in Acts and of Paul in his own letters.

Toward the end of Luke's second book Theophilus comes to an event in the ministry of Apollos, another significant figure (1 Cor 1:12; 3:4–6; 16:12; Titus 3:13). While he spoke and taught accurately, being well-versed in the scriptures, he nevertheless needed further instruction (Acts 18:24–26). Priscilla and Aquila took him aside and expounded the way of God to him more accurately (*akribesteron*). Here we have a clear example of an eloquent Christian man being taught by a woman, Priscilla, and Aquila. The connotation of such instruction of Apollos suggests that this husband and wife team (Acts 18:2), Jewish Christians who were not converts of Paul and who served a church in their houses in both Ephesus and Rome, were regarded by Luke—and probably by others within past Christian leadership—as theological teachers.[2]

As a New Testament scholar it is my contention that an unreal picture of Peter, Paul, and Apollos that is inculcated by a subcultural worldview based on the "apostolic-age" style of interpretation retards the enterprise of global evangelism. These are significant New Testament figures whose life settings and voices should be allowed to speak clearly to the mission of taking the gospel to the ends of the earth. Instead, their authentic characterization and personification rendered by Luke is often muffled and beclouded to suit the contemporary religious custom of some and the desire to preserve the chasmal extinguishment of spiritual giftedness

2. So too, Eisen, *Amtsträgerinnen im frühen Christentum*, 107–108.

and women's ministries. This must be serious to God and his plan and purpose for all humankind. Half the potential workforce God is counting on for world evangelism is eliminated, stifled, and squelched because of a strange doctrine manufactured and maintained by a past socio-philosophical tradition—with no disrespect to Christian philosophers— that apparently continues to be overimpressed by its own cultural and secular norms.

I hope I may not be too bold in suggesting that perhaps those who continue to propagate this questionable and potentially unreal picture of New Testament characters, doing so in an unthoughtful and deliberate manner, might prepare to give an account of themselves in the afterlife, given that it appears to be against the plan and purpose of God and the activity of the Spirit from the heavenly Jesus that is clearly visible in Luke-Acts. All of Paul's prior writings, perhaps especially his letter to the Romans, are also quite unharmonious with this false picture, in my opinion. I would suggest that neither Theophilus nor Luke nor any Christian Greco-Roman student of Paul, whether male or female, could read Paul's occasional correspondence and come away thinking that Paul sought to terminate any of the spiritual activities that he refers to in his discourse or that he sought to terminate women's ministries.

Instead, as to this latter component of a proof-texting style of interprtetation, I would argue that Luke-Acts is a document that God has preserved as a source for Christian theology, pneumatology, and the practice thereof. Before the first Jerusalem Pentecost, Jesus told all those gathered in prayer, including women, to wait for the gift of the Holy Spirit for empowerment to take the Gospel to the remotest part of the earth (Acts 1:4–5, 8, 14). This first example and precedent of Spirit-reception by believer-disciple-witnesses suggests to me that the resurrected Jesus believed, and the heavenly Jesus confirmed (Acts 2:4, 17–18, 33), that

Christian women may expect to be called into the ministry. It is difficult for me to believe that Luke could have written these things unless he also believed this. Aside from just misleading Christians who are called to serve according to a heavenly plan, this aforementioned elimination, stifling, and squelching of women's ministries is a major bone of contention to be laid against the dispensational/cessationistic claims of some.

Obeying the great commission of Jesus is what the global Pentecostal community and the international Charismatic Renewal are primarily engaged in, in one way or another. The contemporary claim by a sector of Protestant Christendom (a minority within world Christendom that is still battling against both the Pentecostal movement and the international Charismatic Renewal because of an ideological attraction rooted in sixteenth-century religious philosophy and debates) that women cannot be missionaries, teachers, preachers, pastors, evangelists, deaconesses, and administrators is to be seriously questioned because it appears to be without biblical foundation. This claim, although venerated by some as traditionally valid, does, in my view, have the potential to work against the Spirit of Jesus, quenching the Spirit's initiatives and thereby causing displeasure to our heavenly Lord.

On the last thought above, regarding the Lord's displeasure, I do not make this statement just because I believe that the Hebrew and Christian Bible is nowhere directly or indirectly supportive of such claims. An additional reason is based on a prophetic revelation I had around three years ago at a friend's home in Atlanta. During our conversation, I had a terrifying and terrible revelation about this. It was shown to me that heaven regards this entire cessationistic doctrine and its insistent truncational corollaries as false and with a terrible displeasure, displeasure akin to death itself. According to this operation of the Holy Spirit, such teaching is dead in heaven. It is now fashionable, and sincerely so, to some here on earth, some within Christendom, but in heaven it is now regarded with great displeasure and considered as death is considered here on earth. While there is no death in heaven, death is understood there. *The dispensational/cessationistic worldview is dead in heaven.* This is the emphatic message of a New Testament prophecy that I must now submit here for communal judgment and discernment according to Paul's procedural guideline (1 Cor 14:29b).[3]

While dogmatics constraining and eliminating spiritual phenomena and women's ministries might once have served some ecclesiastical and/or political purpose in the distant past, it could be a matter of speculation as to whether it ever served God as he desires to be served. I can and do appreciate political considerations and human weaknesses, so far be it from me to foolishly sit in judgment upon Christians past and present. However, what I can say, based upon what happened to me, is that now this theory is considered dead in heaven. I realize that it is not normative for a scholar to share something like this, but I am trusting the Holy Spirit to wisely do with this what he wills. The revelation was so terrible I had to talk through it with several colleagues before I really understood it. I was made to feel how heaven feels about this group of claims; I was given a human feeling of *death and utter disgust*. I interpret this to mean that this is how the powers in heaven feel and think now about these uncritical claims that mislead humankind and thwart divine calling. There is nothing on earth that I know of that I can compare to this. Please allow me to state that this revelation did not originate with me at all. It was so overwhelming that I had to actually sit down. It was almost too much to bear. I could relate this to how Peter probably

3. I trust that my submission for judgment also accords with the consensus of opinion to be found, for example, in Ellis, "Prophecy."

felt (Acts 5:9) when he prophesied that the person he was looking at was going to die. That probably did not make Peter feel good. I suspect that what I was given was worse than that.

5

Romans and Related Observations

WHAT PAUL reveals about his personal attitude toward women's ministry in his letter to the Romans, complementing what we have already seen in Paul's other letters and in the account of Peter, Paul and Apollos in Luke-Acts, suggests that there is a good deal to be learned here. Ongoing study of diverse literary documents and letters originating in the Greco-Roman world where Paul lived and wrote also sheds new light on the social and historical contexts. This background information is significant for a charism-sensitive interpretive method. It helps to illuminate a world wherein Greek-speaking and Latin-speaking Christian people, empowered by the Holy Spirit, communicated to one another and ministered with each other, independent of gender, ethnicity, and social class, to evangelize the known world and build the Christian community.

Paul's letter to the Romans shows that Paul appreciates the patroness Phoebe (Rom 16:1–2), probably a supporter of the missionary enterprise. She served in the church at Cenchrea near Rome. We do not know what form her patronage took, but there were undoubtedly many needs. For example, in the literary community in Rome with its libraries, book dealers, and house churches there could have been a need to support the copying of selected texts, sermons, letters, and Jesus material. In any case, however, Phoebe (*phoibe*) was directly assisting in the missionary enterprise as a patroness (*not* a "helper," a stodgy translation of the feminine Greek word for patroness, *prostatis*); Paul regards her very highly and notes that she is a deaconess in a local church. The Greek word Paul employs (*diakonos*) should be rightly translated into English as "deacon" or as "deaconess," and it is properly rendered as such in a number of culturally sensitive translations in the world's known languages. For example, in today's gospel outreach more than seven hundred Pentecostal organizations and their missionaries involved in world evangelism in many of the world's languages normatively ordain and/or recognize deaconesses in their churches, Spirit-filled women who can preach, teach, administrate, occasionally copastor if needed, and supervise the multiplication of gospel workers. Phoebe's ministries were highly appreciated by Paul in a similar vein as both a patroness and a deaconess.[1]

The Greek language here is unequivocal about this fact. Languages age and change and may eventually die, but the meaning of their words does not. The world of past languages can be understood. Phoebe was a patroness and a deaconess in a local church. She was highly regarded and respected for her service and she was remembered as well. She must have set a good example in her ministry, one that was probably deemed worthy of imitation by others. We have a Christian tombstone in Jerusalem from the fourth century with a cross and an inscription that praises the deceased as having exemplified the deaconess Phoebe from Rome in her own life: "Here lies the slave and bride of Christ, Sophia, deaconess, the second Phoibe, who fell asleep in peace on the 21st of the month of March."[2]

---

1. Jewett, *Romans*, 941–48, provides a thorough discussion of Rom 16:1–3.

2. Horsley, "Sophia, the Second Phoibe," 239.

Next, we note that at Romans 16:3–5a, Paul extends his greetings to and acknowledges Prisca and Aquila as "my fellow workers in Christ Jesus," who ministered to the church in their house. Aquila and his wife, whom Luke calls Priscilla (Acts 18:2, 18, 26), evidently had money to travel and acquire property. They were fellow workers with Paul and established churches in Ephesus and then in Rome. When Paul writes his letter to the Romans from Corinth, he knows that Prisca and Aquila (their Latin names) are ministering in Rome. Their movements within the Empire contribute to the impression that the various Christian communities were in touch with one another and, further, that through this travel important Christian documents were also probably circulated among churches to be read aloud.

The Greek word for "fellow worker" (*sunergos*, Rom 16:3) in this context conveys the meaning of being missionary colleagues. The expression here (*sunergos*) is a rather unique Pauline expression and actually refers to persons who work together with Paul as "agents of God"[3] in the common work of missionary preaching and teaching. Both Prisca and Aquila are regarded as such persons by Paul, that is, as missionary colleagues and fellow agents of God engaged in collaborative pastoral work. The expression translated "fellow workers"[4] has the connotation of sharing a divine commission and does not merely imply that Prisca and Aquila are helpers of the apostle. They are working together as partners *in Christ Jesus*.

---

3. Ollrog, *Paulus und siene Mitarbeiter*, 67. The term "fellow worker" is used of personal associates of Paul who exercised various ministries, including teaching, preaching, and prophecy. This would include Titus (2 Cor 8:23), Mark (Col 4:10–11), Timothy (1 Thess 3:2; Rom 16:21), and Prisca and Aquila (Rom 16:3), among others. Euodia and Syntyche, women who labored side by side with Paul, are probably to be included under Paul's collaborative identification of "fellow workers" (Phil 4:3).

4. Ollrog, "*sunergos, sunergeō*."

They are in the same service. The clear implication of Paul's distinctive language here is that each one, namely Prisca and Aquila, functions as a missionary who "becomes a colleague and coworker with Paul, who is called to the same task as Paul and in the same service of preaching to build faith in the . . . congregation."[5] This is how the real Paul recognizes, understands, and appreciates Prisca and Aquila.

The practice of copastoring as a husband and wife team is very common today in global Pentecostalism throughout most countries of the world based upon this particular model. A husband and wife serving as missionary copastors of storefront churches in inner cities among the poor or in churches in cities in India, Mexico, or Tennessee, for example, means that they share the ministry of pastoral care including counseling, visitation, prayer, teaching, and preaching.

At Romans 16:3, we note that Prisca's name appears first. She is mentioned before her husband. Also, after their introduction into Luke's narrative at Acts 18:2, we then see that Luke, using the more conversational Priscilla, twice places her name first (Acts 18:18a, 26b), perhaps agreeing with Paul's previous usage in Romans. It may be that Paul and Luke refer to her in this way to indicate that she has a higher social status than her husband. She may have come from a noble Roman family background (the gens Prisca). There is some evidence for that connection based on records of Roman nobility. When a woman's name is mentioned first in Greek texts, before her husband's, there is usually a reason. Mentioning her name first in this instance (Rom 16:3) would not necessarily mean that she was more active in ministry than her husband, but that in Rome, the capital of the known world where social status mattered and was appreciated as a fact of life, her status was so recognized by politely mentioning her name first.

5. Ollrog, *Paulus und siene Mitarbeiter*, 72.

To continue to casually deny to such a person as Prisca (Priscilla), as well as the aforementioned Phoebe the deaconess, the Spirit-directed service of ministering in Roman churches via preaching, teaching, and codirecting missionary work is without textual merit and appears to rely more on a tradition than on evidence. The imposition of such a paradigm appears to propagate a religious philosophy of women's role in society stemming from the world of the Protestant Reformers. Obviously, the modern dispensational/cessationistic or "apostolic-age" paradigm with its proclivity to truncate a full range of women's ministries and spiritual enablements cannot be successfully imposed upon Paul's understanding of either Phoebe or Prisca, just as it cannot be imposed upon Paul's view of Christian prophetesses in Corinth or his fellowship with Philip's prophesying daughters in Acts. The invocation of this paradigm today appears to be an unlikely Evangelical Protestant project that is in need of scriptural questioning. This critically unexamined creedal mixture functions to insensitively marginalize women in their Spirit-directed ministries for convenient reasons of preserving ecclesiastical tradition and/or male power, while at the same time failing to get into the textual details of biblical evidence.

Continuing with our analysis, Paul asks that the Roman tenement and house churches greet Andronikos and Junia on his behalf (Rom 16:7), "Greet Andronikos and Junia, my compatriots and my fellow prisoners, who are outstanding among the apostles, who were begotten in Christ even before me."[6] Junia is a feminine Latin name. Some two hundred and fifty examples of that name have been found in Roman documents. The evidence showing that "Junia" is a common feminine name is overwhelming. Not a single example of a masculine name "Junias" has ever been found. That this Junia is a woman is beyond dispute. "Junia" is the correct translation of the Greek name Paul writes.

Paul writes the name "Junian" here in the Greek accusative case (*Iounian*), because the name is the direct object of the verb "greet." However, when the name is expressed in the Greek manner whereby people are directly called by their name, the Greek nominative or vocative case would be used. Accordingly, in this event, the name of this person could be either "Junia" (feminine) or "Junias" (masculine). If "Junia," the person in Romans 16:7 would be a woman, if "Junias," the person would be a man. One has to investigate Greco-Roman names to find out. This now has been thoroughly done.[7] To reiterate, the result is that very many people named "Junia" have been found. They are all women. Not a single person named "Junias," who would be a man, has ever been found. This indicates clearly that "Junias" did not exist as a name for a man. Therefore, the person Paul identifies here in 16:7 by the common name "Junia" is a woman.

Martin Luther incorrectly popularized the masculine option for this name and the worldview of the fifteenth

---

6. Here I follow the excellent translation of Jewett, *Romans*, 949. Replacing the traditional "kinsmen" with the translation "compatriots" seems better suited to the spirit of collaboration in a common divine calling and it eliminates the wrongful implication of ancestry, as I note in the next section of this present study. Translating *gegonan* in the final clause as "were begotten" instead of "were" or "have been" seems better suited to how Paul and his compatriots would probably think of themselves as appearing in their own history of distinctive Christian experience.

7. Belleville, "*Iounian*;" Epp, *Junia*.

century could easily absorb such scholarly assurance that women could not be ministers, because to say this would be too big of a break from the Catholic church, which had in a number of respects gone astray. Luther did not want a woman to be an apostle, as Paul identified Junia, much less an outstanding one. If he recognized that, then he would have to allow women to be priests. As a former Catholic priest, Luther came from a tradition where only men could be priests. Almost every other translator and commentator until the end of the twentieth century followed Luther and treated this female apostle as a man simply on the basis of sexist presupposition. Perhaps Junia being a woman may have been too revolutionary, and so she and her accomplishments remained in eclipse without investigation. This did seem to fit amiably into the status quo of some. Luther and the other Reformers, in generally truncating the applicability of the miraculous, did not totally break off from their opponents. They retained infant baptism, which was later discarded by some, and they retained the contemporary cultural worldview about women in general—a worldview unharmonious with Spirit-empowered *Christian* women in first-century Christianity as reflected in New Testament documents.

Inkwells from the Scriptorium at Qumran

6

Romans in Light of
Modern Translation Methods

A HUNDRED years after Luther, flowing from the
Protestant Reformation, a translation committee was
assembled in England by the British king, James, at the beginning of the seventeenth century. James was sympathetic
to extending Protestant power within the British Empire
and serving English Protestants with a translation bearing
his name. James was also a king whom the Irish people
to this day generally regard as a usurper and an exploiter
of poor and godly Christians from another faith tradition
for his own political gain. His committee, perhaps accommodating, or at least unduly influenced by, male Protestant
tradition toward women, hastily turned Junia into a man
without investigation by simply labeling Andronikus and
Junia at Romans 16:7 as "kinsmen." The fact that "Junia"
sounds and feels like a woman's name to someone familiar
with the Greek language—perhaps something that could
have suggested itself to the king's committee—may have
been overlooked or brushed aside as a nonstarter, just as
this also appears to have been done by some subsequent
translation committees who had more Greek texts at their
fingertips. The fact that "Junias," the other Greek alternative, although perhaps sounding like a man's name, did not
correspond to any known man in the Greco-Roman world
might also have occasioned a pause, or at least have been

thought worth looking into. It might be suggested that the king's committee ignored these serious issues and instead produced a deferential and uninvestigated translation of "my kinsmen" at Romans 16:7, without question turning this person into a man based on no evidence whatsoever. In any case, as pointed out in the previous chapter of this present study, authentic research has now shown that the person "Junia" in 16:7 is a woman, specifically a female apostle.

Just to review, Junia is a feminine Latin name; Junias is not known to be a man's name. These facts are obtained through research and reading of the many personal, civic, and commercial letters written in Greek and preserved from the time immediately before, during, and after the first century. For example, Luke's double work is addressed to a person named Theophilus (Luke 1:3; Acts 1:1) who is undoubtedly a man. If Luke had written "Theophila," then it would be necessary to read some of these extant letters and see if other people therein had this feminine-sounding Greek name. If one does this, as I have, one finds a number of men named "Theophilus" and women named "Theophila." Just as a "Theophila," had Luke written that name, should not be turned into a "Theophilus" for political or cultural reasons, so too, a "Junia" should not be turned into a man named "Junias" for such reasons. Further, in this case, a determining and undeniable factor precluding such a transformation and misidentification is that, although many women had the name "Junia," there is no historical evidence for the existence of any man named "Junias."

This procedure of uninvestigated sex change or gender erasure may be somewhat understandable within temporally changing ecclesiastical conditions, but *not* for the ongoing task of accurate translation. Several other people in the context of Romans 16:7 are also identified by the same Greek word (*suggenēs*) that the early seventeenth-century British translation committee rendered either as "kinsman" or the plural "kinsmen." "Kinsmen" would obviously be the wrong translation at 16:7 if the person Paul cites here is indeed a woman, *which we now are very confident is the case.* "Kinsmen" would also be wrong unless it can be believed Paul is signaling that he means these other people were his ethnic kinfolk according to the flesh (as at Rom 9:3).

There is no hint in this context that Paul is ethnically related to Andronikos, Junia, Herodian (Rom 16:11), or to Lucius or Jason or Sosipater (16:21), all people for whom Paul uses this same Greek word to identify. It should not be taken to mean ethnic relative because its usage here also suggests a narrower and particular *Christian* connotation of collaboration within the revolutionary social equality in Christ. Therefore, it seems highly unlikely that Paul is identifying these people as his ethnic kinfolk, but rather as joint participants in a new spiritual community, and a more sensitive translation can reflect Paul's probable meaning. It seems clear that this Greek word (*suggenēs*) is preferably not to be rendered here as "kinsman" or its plural "kinsmen," but *instead* as "compatriots" in 16:7, 21 or as "compatriot" when singular, as in 16:11. *The relationship between Paul and these individuals is not biological kinship; rather it is experiential relationship of being spiritual compatriots in ministry in Christ Jesus.*

Unfortunately oft repeated, the king's translation committee's use of "kinsmen" at 16:7, 21 and "kinsman" at 16:11—based as it was on a decision that the Greek word (*suggenēs*) would be translated by them in such a way that the female "Junia" was erased in order to create "Junias" as a man *and* an ethnic relative of Paul—was based on no research and missed the boat on both points. In deference to their task and their era, we should recognize that the working principles for preparing a translation were in their infancy. Nevertheless, their performance in this regard has misled many unsuspecting people, but now, I suggest, this boat can finally be righted.

To recap, and this is important given that wrong or biased translations leave lasting impressions, Greek translation committees could easily suspect that "Junia" was a feminine name and that "Junias" did not seem to be an obvious, known masculine name. The fact that some, perhaps mistakenly following King James' committee, translate *diakonos* at Romans 16:1 as "servant" rather than deacon or deaconess also suggests an ongoing translation bias against women (corrected by the RSV and the NJB). Deacon or deaconess is the closest natural English equivalent to *diakonos*. Verbal consistency in translating *diakonos* throughout Paul's writings—*not* just when men are in view—is preferable to possibly importing later cultural, secular, or ecclesiastical assumptions into the text that could lead to misleading and unhistorical translations. Translation committees might also easily suspect that "Junia" could *not* be a "kinsman." They might venture a guess that "Junia" appears to be a feminine name *and* they would know that they had never seen any man in Greek literature identified by the name "Junias." However, these factors somehow managed to be overlooked for several centuries. That an outstanding apostle could be a woman, equal in that respect with a man, or that a woman could be a deaconess, again equivalent in that respect with a man, perhaps went against the social and political outlook of some, although it complements a distinctive first-century Christian understanding of women's ministry that may be reasonably deduced from Luke's portrayals of Peter, Paul, and Apollos as well as from Paul's letters.

On most other translation accounts, but not all, the first Protestant translation committee's work, both employing and highly imitating the earlier unpolished translation done by William Tyndale in its use of Shakespearean English words, was good for its time. It is a venerated English trans-

lation. However, more accurate translations with more accurate renderings of many Greek words, well-suited to more
accurate preaching, have now replaced it based on our much
better understanding of New Testament Greek *and*, impor-
tantly as well, on major discoveries of much earlier—and
therefore generally more reliable—New Testament manuscripts that were not available until the nineteenth century.
The earlier (older) the manuscript, the closer it is to the time
of the original writing. These large and beautifully preserved
manuscripts of the Greek New Testament, copied from
earlier papyrus documents onto more permanent animal
skins in the fourth and fifth centuries, were not available to
translators at the beginning of the seventeenth century. At
that time translators only had much later manuscripts from
which to work, manuscripts which were farther removed in
time from their authorship. These and other more recent
discoveries yield a significantly improved Greek text from
which to prepare translations in the world's languages.

To serve the need of Bible translators throughout the
world with an edition of the Greek New Testament that takes
the several hundred known New Testament documents into
account so as to properly prepare the most accurate and the
most faithful text from which translators may work, an alli-
ance of Bible societies was formed. To accomplish the task
of preparing the best text of the Greek New Testament for
translators and their eventual readers, a number of Bible societies that were already active in translation and missionary
work joined forces. The United Bible Societies now comprise
the following groups: the National Bible Society of Scotland
(Edinburgh), the American Bible Society (New York), the
Württemberg Bible Society (Stuttgart, Germany—taking their name from Württemberg, the city where Martin
Luther began the Protestant Reformation in 1517), and The
Netherlands Bible Society (Amsterdam, Holland).

The United Bible Societies then collaborate further with a research institute in Germany, the Institute for New Testament Textual Research (located in Münster, North Rhine-Westphalia). The result of all this joint and detailed cooperation is a Greek New Testament that serves the world's languages and peoples. Many of the world's languages have a translation prepared from this Greek text, with some languages, like English, having more than one. However, some languages still await translations that can serve in missionary work. This important ministry is, in part, the commendable work of Wycliffe translators, John Wycliffe being the first scholar to translate the four Gospels from Latin into English in the fourteenth century. William Tyndale, whose more modern English translation with Shakespearean overtones from Greek manuscripts also preceded King James' translation committee, was martyred in 1536—burned at the stake—for his translation work. While the king's committee appears to have been influenced by Tyndale's translation in a significant number of instances, it seems evident that they decided not to follow the spirit of his translation at Romans 16:1 and 7: "I commede unto you Phebe oure sister (which is a minister of the congregacion of Chenchrea)" and "Salute Andronicus and Iunia my cosyns which were presoners with me also which are wele taken amoge the Apostles and were in Christ before me."

Returning to our textual analysis, Andronikos and Junia (Rom 16:7), are not only *compatriots*, but also "my fellow prisoners," Paul writes. The choice of this expression (*sunaichmalōtos*, fellow prisoners) would resonate with readers who could have been exposed to a misuse of Roman military or political power. It implies a shared struggle in ministry that missionaries and pastors especially understand. Those who struggle today against pejorative and demeaning labels based on an inadequate interpretive method and secular gender bias may find solace and inclusion in Paul's metaphor of "fellow prisoner" in Christ.

The next expression Paul employs to describe Andronikos and Junia, "outstanding among the apostles" (Rom 16:7) is revealing. The adjective "outstanding" lifts up a person or thing as distinguished or marked in comparison with other representatives of the same class, in this instance the other apostles. It might also be properly translated as "notable among the apostles." Paul's expression "outstanding (or notable) among the apostles" is an English translation expressing what he really has in mind. *Paul means here that among the apostles he is acquainted with, Andronikos and Junia were thought of as being outstanding apostles.*

This is the historical Paul speaking his mind. One of the keen commentators of the fourth century, a Greek speaker himself, famously said of Andronikos and Junia: "Even to be an apostle is great, but to be prominent among them—consider how wonderful a song of honor that is." (John Chrysostom, *Homily on Romans*, 31.2).

Some twenty-nine references to persons with the name of Andronikos have been discovered in Rome. The Christian Andronikos was probably a resident there. Andronikos and Junia, ministers Paul himself believed to be outstanding apostles, known to be regarded as outstanding apostles by other apostles, are said to be "also in Christ before me" (Rom 16:7). This means that they were known to be Christians before Paul was converted and filled with the Holy Spirit and baptized via Ananias' ministry (Acts 9:3–18). Andronikos and Junia had functioned in their ministry for more than two decades before Paul wrote his letter to the Romans (as we can deduce from the dates associated with Paul's life in Acts and from various statements in his letters that Romans was written from Corinth in 56–57 CE). Could they have been among the one hundred and twenty (Acts 1:14–15) at the first Jerusalem Pentecost? Among the five hundred (1 Cor

15:6)? Such speculation must remain unanswered, but they appear to be highly regarded. Paul now requests (Rom 16:7) that Andronikos and Junia be greeted by other believers in Rome who were evidently inclined to acknowledge and respect their accomplishments. *Deaconess Phoebe and copastor Prisca, as well as the outstanding apostle Junia, served our Lord in heaven-ordained ministries that were recognized and appreciated by Paul and by many others.* Similarly, and equally to be appreciated and greeted with honor are Tryphaina and Tryphosa (Rom 16:12), "laborers in the Lord," and the beloved Persis (Persis being a female slave name of Persian origin) who "labored much in the Lord," suggesting that these three women were also missionaries or local church leaders with whom Paul must have been personally acquainted.

Conclusion

So, DEAR Theo, I hope that these thoughts and observations may be helpful to you in your ministry as you pursue your calling as a Spirit-filled servant who continues to reflect and consider. I trust also that the Select Bibliography that follows will be of assistance to you as well in delving into the details underpinning this letter. I encourage you to get into the details concerning the issues that have been raised. There is nothing like a focused bibliography to point a student in the right direction and stimulate further investigation. Biblical theology is serious work and requires patience. Perhaps the assurance and guidance you may have gained from the present letter will give you something to build on.

Contextual interpretation that seeks real continuity with the Christians characterized and personified in our New Testament documents, not uncritical allegiance to unexamined assumptions, offers the best opportunity to be harmonious with the theological and pneumatological intentions of intelligent authors who desire to influence their original and later readers. It will also be important to recognize that it is the Holy Spirit who represents the presence of the Lord Jesus Christ in this world. This active presence should be sought, respected, evaluated, and cherished because the Holy Spirit will want to support real continuity with the examples and precedents of Christian experience that New Testament writers describe.

Your desire now to obtain ministerial credentials for hospital and nursing home visitation and for occasional preaching is very admirable. May your wife stand by your side in this lifelong endeavor as you continue to work with all those whom our God has called into his service. When attempting to comfort others and to preach with the Holy Spirit sent down from heaven (1 Pet 1:12b), I sincerely hope that the heavenly Jesus will give you the desire to edify, strengthen, and truthfully inform so that your hearers may grow spiritually and experientially in the grace and knowledge of our Lord Jesus Christ.

I would like to share in conclusion two sentiments and then a scripture given to me upon my ordination amidst the prayers of compatriots at Bethel Tabernacle Pentecostal, Detroit, Michigan, on July 25, 1971. I received a number of lovely sentiments that day. I still treasure them. Here is one: "God bless the day your vows are made. His wisdom guide you unafraid throughout the tasks you start this day of leading others in His way!" This is signed as follows: "Always in His Service, with love until He calls me home or comes for me. Mary E. Matthews, ordained Minister, Evangelist and Missionary, working in all three areas." Here is another: "God bless you on this special event; as we all know it is God who ordains, but as all things are done for good to those who love the Lord, our prayer is that this event will uplift you in your future (present too) ministry, reconciling others unto Christ as this ministry is given to us (2 Cor 5:18–19), always taking heed as mentioned in Col 4:17. The Lord bless you my brother, . . . Jerry." Paul's urgent exhortation to Archippus was "See that you fulfill the ministry which you received in the Lord" (Col 4:17). Unworthy as I am, I have found this thought to be excellent advice for staying on the battlefield. Perhaps it will serve you well when your divine commission is confirmed by our fellow servants and you go on to regions beyond. I hope this occasion will be a blessed day for you as it was for me. God bless you, my good brother!

May the Holy Spirit lead and guide you in God's purposes,
Your friend,
Brother Paul

Select Bibliography

Abrahamsen, Valerie A. *Women and Worship at Philippi: Diana/Artemis and Other Cults in the Early Christian Era*. Portland, OR: Astarte Shell, 1995.

Aland, Barbara, et al., editors. *The Greek New Testament*. 4th edition. New York/London/ Edinburg/Amsterdam/Württemberg/ Münster: United Bible Societies/Institute for New Testament Textual Research, 1994.

Alexander, Estrelda. *The Women of Azusa Street*. Cleveland, OH: Pilgrim, 2005.

Alexander, Kimberly. "Women in the Ministry of Healing—The Rise of Itinerant Healing Evangelists." In *Pentecostal Healing: Models in Theology and Practice*, 176–86. JPTSup. Blandford Forum, Dorset: Deo, 2006.

Alexander, Kimberly, and R. Hollis Gause. *Women in Leadership: A Pentecostal Perspective*. Center for Pentecostal Leadership and Care. Cleveland, TN: Church of God Theological Seminary, 2006.

Amstutz, John. "Beyond Pentecost: A Study of Some Sociological Dimensions of New Testament Church Growth from the Book of Acts." In *Essays on Apostolic Themes: Studies in Honor of Howard M. Ervin*, edited by Paul Elbert, 208–25. Eugene, OR: Wipf & Stock, 2007.

Anderson, Graham. "Greek Religion in the Roman Empire: Diversities, Convergences, Uncertainties." In *Religious Diversity in the Graeco-Roman World: A Survey of Recent Scholarship*, edited by Dan Cohn-Sherbok and John M. Court, 143–63. Biblical Seminar 79. Sheffield: Sheffield Academic Press, 2001.

Archer, Kenneth J. "Critique of the Evangelical Historical Critical Method." In *A Pentecostal Hermeneutic for the Twenty-First Century: Spirit, Scripture and Community*, 148–54. JPTSup 28. London: T & T Clark, 2004.

———. "A Pentecostal Way of Doing Theology: Method and Manner." *IJST* 9 (2007) 301–14.

Barth, Markus. "Husband and Wife." In *Ephesians 4–6: A New Translation with Introduction and Commentary*, 700–15. AB 43A. Garden City, NY: Doubleday, 1974.

———. "The Problem of Hidden Persuaders." In "Christ and All Things," *Paul and Paulinism: Essays in honour of C. K. Barrett*, edited by M. D. Hooker and S. G. Wilson, 160–72 (164–68). London: SPCK, 1982.

Beard, Mary, et al. *Religions of Rome*. 2 vols. Cambridge: Cambridge University Press, 1998.

Belleville, Linda L. *Women Leaders and the Church*. Grand Rapids, MI: Baker, 2000.

———. "*Iounian . . . episē moi en tois apostolois*: a re-examination of Romans 16.7 in light of primary source materials." *NTS* 51 (2005) 231–49.

Benvenuti, Sherilyn. "Anointed, Gifted and Called: Pentecostal Women in Ministry." *Pneuma: Journal of the Society for Pentecostal Studies* 17 (1991) 229–35.

Berlin, Adele. "A Search for a New Biblical Hermeneutics: Preliminary Observations." In *The Study of the Ancient Near East in the Twenty-First Century: The William Foxwell Albright Centennial Conference*, edited by J. S. Cooper and G. M. Schwartz, 195–207. Winona Lake, IN: Eisenbrauns, 1996.

Blank, Josef, et al., editors. *Die Frau im Urchristentum*. QD 95. 4th edition. Freiburg, Herder, 1989.

Bookidis, Nancy. "Religion in Corinth: 140BCE to 100CE." In *Urban Religion in Roman Corinth: Interdisciplinary Approaches*, edited by Daniel N. Schowalter and Steven J Friesen, 141–64. Harvard Theological Studies 53. Cambridge, MA: Harvard University Press, 2005.

Brodie, Thomas L. "Towards Tracing the Gospel's Literary Indebtedness to the Epistles." In *Mimesis and Intertextuality in Antiquity and Christianity*, edited by Dennis R. MacDonald, 104–16. Studies in Antiquity & Christianity. Harrisburg, PA: Trinity, 2001.

Brooten, Bernadette J. "'Junia . . . Outstanding among the Apostles' (Romans 16:7)." In *Women Priests: A Catholic Commentary on the Vatican Declaration*, edited by Leonard J. and Arlene Swidler, 141–44. New York: Paulist, 1977.

———. *Women Leaders in the Ancient Synagogue: Inscriptional Evidence and Background Issues*. BJS 36. Chico, CA: Scholars, 1982.

Buchanan, Colin, et al., *The Charismatic Movement in the Church of England*. London: CIO, 1981.

Butler, Anthea D. *Women in the Church of God in Christ: Making a Sanctified World*. Chapel Hill, NC: University of North Carolina Press, 2007.

Calvin, John. *Commentariorum Joannis Calvini in Acts Apostolorum, I*. Geneva: Ex officina Ioannis Crispini, 1552.

Cavaness, Barbara. "God Calling: Women in Pentecostal Missions." In *Azusa Street & Beyond: 100 Years of Commentary on the Global Pentecostal/Charismatic Movement*, edited by Grant McClung, 53–66. Gainesville, FL: Bridge-Logos, 2006.

Christian, Ed. "Women, Teaching, Authority, Silence: 1 Timothy 2:8–15 Explained by 1 Peter 3:1–6." *Journal of the Adventist Theological Society* 10 (1999) 285–90.

Colijn, Brenda B. "A Biblical Theology of Women in Leadership." *ATJ* 34 (2002) 67–80.

Daniels, David. "Until the Power of the Lord Comes Down: African American Pentecostal Spirituality and Tarrying." In *Contemporary Spiritualities: Social and Religious Contexts*, edited by Clive Erricker and Jane Erricker, 173–91. London: Continuum, 2001.

Davidson, Richard. "Headship, Submission, and Equality." In *Women in Ministry: Biblical and Historical Perspectives*, edited by Nancy Vyhmister, 259–95. Berrien Springs, MI: Andrews University Press, 1998.

———. *Flame of Yahweh: Sexuality in the Old Testament*. Peabody, MA: Hendrickson, 2007.

Eisen, Ute E. *Amtsträgerinnen im frühen Christentum: Epigraphische und literarische Studien*. FKDG 61. Göttingen, Vandenhoeck & Ruprecht, 1996.

———. "Methodologische Grundlegung der Narratologie." In *Die Poetik der Apostelgeschichte: Eine narratologische Studie*, 44–139. NTOA/SUNT 58. Fribourg: Academic Press/Göttingen: Vandenhoeck & Ruprecht, 2006.

Elbert, Paul. "The Charismatic Movement in the Church of England: An Overview." *Pneuma: Journal of the Society for Pentecostal Studies* 6/1 (1984) 27–50.

———. "Calvin and the Spiritual Gifts" In *An Elaboration of the Theology of Calvin: Articles on Calvin and Calvinism, VIII*, edited by Richard C. Gamble, 303–31. New York: Garland, 1992.

———. "The Globalization of Pentecostalism: A Review Article." *TrinJ* NS23 (2002) 81–101. Accessed October 1, 2007. Online: http://www.pneumafoundation.com/resources/articles/review.guest0002.pdf.

———. "Pentecostal/Charismatic Themes in Luke-Acts at the Evangelical Theological Society: The Battle of Interpretive Method." *JPT* 12 (2004) 181–215. Accessed October 1, 2007. Online: http://www.pneumafoundation.org/resources/articles/JPT_PentChar Themes.pdf.

———. "Luke's Fulfillment of Prophecy Theme: Introductory Exploration of Joel and the Last Days." Presented to the Society for Pentecostal Studies, Marquette University, 2004. Accessed October 1, 2007. Online: http://www.tffps.org/resources.htm#articles_reviews.

———. "Paul of the Miletus Speech and 1 Thessalonians: Critique and Considerations." *ZNW* 95 (2004) 258–68.

———. "An Observation on Luke's Composition and Narrative Style of Questions." *CBQ* 66 (2004) 98–109.

———. "Possible Literary Links Between Luke-Acts and Paul's Letters Regarding Spirit-Language." In *Intertextuality in the New Testament: Explorations of Theory and Practice*, edited by Thomas L. Brodie et al., 226–54. New Testament Monographs 16. Sheffield; Sheffield-Phoenix, 2006.

———. "Toward A Pentecostal Hermeneutic: Observations on Archer's Progressive Proposal." *Asian Journal of Pentecostal Studies* 9 (2006) 320–28.

———. "The Potential of a 'Charism-Sensitive or Pentecostal/Charismatic Narrative-Critical Method' with Greco-Roman Progymnasmatic Affinities." In "Narrative-Rhetorical Aspects of Literary Hermeneutics: Leaving Questionable Methods Behind and Retaining what Greco-Roman Christian Writers Appreciated and Respected." *Refleks: Med Karismatisk Kristendom i Focus* 6 (2007), 89–131 (126–31).

Ellis, E. Earle. "Prophecy in the New Testament Church—and Today." In *Prophetic Vocation in the New Testament and Today*, edited by J. Panagopoulos, 46–57. NovTSup 45. Leiden: Brill, 1977.

———. "'Spiritual Gifts' in the Pauline Community." In *Prophecy and Hermeneutic in Early Christianity: New Testament Essays*, 23–44. WUNT 2/18. Tübingen: Mohr, 1978.

———. "Paul and the Eschatological Woman." In *Pauline Theology: Ministry and Society*, 53–86. Lanham, MD: University Press of America, 1997.

Epp, Eldon Jay. "Text-critical, Exegetical, and Socio-cultural Factors Affecting the Junia/Junias Variation in Romans 16:7." In *New Testament Textual Criticism and Exegesis: Festschrift Joël Delobel*, edited by Adelbert Denaux, 227–91. BETL 161. Leuven: Leuven University Press, 2002.

———. *Junia: The First Woman Apostle*. Minneapolis: Fortress, 2005.

Fee, Gordon D. *God's Empowering Presence: The Holy Spirit in the Letters of Paul*. Peabody, MA: Hendrickson, 1994.

Ferguson, John. *The Religions of the Roman Empire*. Aspects of Greek and Roman Life. Ithaca: Cornell University Press, 1970.

Fiorenza, Elisabeth Schüssler. "Missionaries, Apostles, Coworkers: Rom 16 and the Reconstruction of Women's Early Christian History." *Word and World* 6 (1986) 420–33.

Fischer, Imtraud. *Women Who Wrestled with God: Biblical Stories of Israel's Beginnings*. Translated by Linda M. Maloney. Collegeville, MN: Liturgical, 2005.

Gause, R. Hollis. "Issues in Pentecostalism." In *Perspectives on the New Pentecostalism*, edited by Russell P. Spittler, 106–16. Grand Rapids, MI: Baker, 1976.

———. *Living in the Spirit: The Way of Salvation*. Revised and expanded version self-published, 2006. Available from the author at 3620 Belmont Cir., NW, Cleveland, TN 37312.

Giles, Kevin. "Women in the Church: A Rejoinder to Andreas Köstenberger." *EQ* 73 (2001) 225–45.

Gill, Deborah M., and Barbara Cavaness. *God's Women—Then and Now*. Springfield, MO: Grace & Truth, 2004. The authors have prepared *A Study to God's Women* in the following languages: Bengali, English, Hindi, Napali, Oriya, and Tamil.

Goldingay, John. "Biblical Story and the Way It Shapes Our Story." *Journal of the European Pentecostal Theological Association* 17 (1997) 5–15.

Graves, Robert W. *Praying in the Spirit*. Old Tappan, NJ: Revell, 1987.

Griffith, R. Marrie, and David Roebuck. "Role of Women." In *New International Dictionary of Pentecostal and Charismatic Movements*, edited by Stanley M. Burgess and Eduard van der Maas, 1203–1209. Grand Rapids, MI: Zondervan, 2002.

Harper, Michael, editor. *Bishops' Move: Six Anglican Bishops Share Their Experience of Renewal*. Foreword by the Archbishop of Canterbury. London: Hodder and Stoughton, 1978.

Haya-Prats, Gonzalo. *L'Esprit, force de l'Église: sa nature et son activité d'après les Actes des apôtres*. LD 81. Paris: Cerf, 1975.

Hicks, Bernice R. *True Worship: In the Demonstrations of the Spirit*. Jeffersonville, IN: Christ Gospel, 1994.

Hocken, Peter. "The Significance and Potential of Pentecostalism." In *New Heaven? New Earth? An Encounter with Pentecostalism*, edited by Simon Tugwell et al., 15–67. Springfield, IL: Templegate, 1977.

Holman, Charles. "Paul's Preaching—Cognitive and Charismatic." In *Spirit and Renewal: Essays in Honor of J. Rodman Williams*, edited by Mark W. Wilson, 143–56. JPTSup 5. Sheffield: Sheffield Academic Press, 1994.

Holmes, Pamela. "'The Place' of Women in Pentecostal/Charismatic Ministry Since the Azusa Street Revival." In *The Azusa Street Revival and Its Legacy*, edited by Cecil M. Robeck, Jr., and Harold D. Hunter, 297–315. Cleveland, TN: Pathway, 2006.

Horsley, G. H. R. "The Purple Trade, and the Status of Lydia of Thyatira." In *New Documents Illustrating Christianity 2*, edited by G. H. R. Horsley, 25–32. Ancient History Documentary Research Centre. New South Wales: Macquarie University Press, 1982.

———. "Sophia, the Second Phoibe." In *New Documents Illustrating Early Christianity 4*, edited by G. H. R. Horsley, 239–44. Ancient History Documentary Research Centre. New South Wales: Macquarie University Press, 1987.

———. "Artemis." In "The Inscriptions of Ephesos and the New Testament." *NovT* 34 (1993) 105–68 (141–58).

Horton, Stanley M. "Spirit Baptism: A Pentecostal Perspective." In *Perspectives on Spirit Baptism, Five Views*, edited by Chad Owen Brand, 47–194. Nashville, TN: Broadman & Holman, 2004.

Hugenberger, Gordon P. "Women in Church Office: Hermeneutics or Exegesis? A Survey of Approaches to 1 Tim 2:8–15." *JETS* 35 (1995) 341–60.

Hyatt, Susan B. "Spirit-Filled Women." In *The Century of the Holy Spirit: 100 Years of Pentecostal and Charismatic Renewal, 1901–2001*, edited by Vinson Synan, 233–63. Nashville, TN: Nelson, 2001. The editor includes eight pages of photographs inserted at page 252.

Jewett, Robert. *Romans*. Hermeneia. Assisted by R. D. Kotansky. Edited by E. J. Epp. Minneapolis: Fortress, 2007.

Johns, Cheryl Bridges. "Pentecostal Spirituality and the Conscientization of Women." In *All Together in One Place: Theological Papers from the Brighton Conference on World Evangelization*, edited by Harold D. Hunter and Peter D. Hocken, 153–65. JPTSup 4. Sheffield: Sheffield Academic Press, 1993.

———. "The Adolescence of Pentecostalism: In Search of a Legitimate Sectarian Identity." *Pneuma: Journal of the Society for Pentecostal Studies* 17 (1995) 3–17.

Judge, E. A. "A Woman's Behaviour." In *New Documents Illustrating Early Christianity 6*, edited by S. R. Llewelyn with the collaboration of R. A. Kearsley, 18–23. Ancient History Documentary Research Centre. New South Wales: Macquarie University Press, 1992.

Kearsley, R. A. "Women in Public Life." In *New Documents Illustrating Early Christianity 6*, edited by S. R. Llewelyn with the collaboration of R. A. Kearsley, 24–27. Ancient History Documentary Research Centre. New South Wales: Macquarie University Press, 1992.

Keener, Craig S. *Paul, Women, Wives: Marriage and Women's Ministry in the Letters of Paul*. Peabody, MA: Hendrickson, 1993.

———. "Learning in the Assemblies: 1 Corinthians 14:34–35." In *Discovering Biblical Equality: Complementarity Without Hierarchy*, edited by Ronald W. Pierce and Rebecca Merrill Groothius, 161–71. Downers Grove, IL: InterVarsity, 2004.

———. "Let the Wife have Authority over her Husband." *JGRChJ* 2 (2001–2005) 146–52.

Klein, Hans. "Paulinische Tradition bei Lukas." In *Lukasstudien*, 13–16. FRLANT 209. Göttingen: Vandenhoeck & Ruprecht, 2005.

———. "Exkurs: Gebet bei Lukas." In *Das Lukasevangelium, I*, 410. KEK 1/3–10. Göttingen: Vandenhoeck & Ruprecht, 2006. Klein demonstrates an onset of methodological sensitivity to narrative continuity in his comments on Luke 3:16; 11:13; 24:49.

Kroeger, Catherine, and Richard Kroeger. *I Suffer Not a Woman: Rethinking 1 Timothy 2:11–15 in Light of Ancient Evidence*. Grand Rapids, MI: Baker, 1992.

Kurz, William S. "Inspiration and the Origins of the New Testament." In *Scripture and the Charismatic Renewal*, edited by George Martin, 29–58. Ann Arbor, MI: Servant, 1979.

van der Laan, Cornelius, "Beyond the Clouds: Elize Scharten (1876–1965), Pentecostal Missionary to China." In *Pentecostalism in Context: Essays in Honor of William W. Menzies*, edited by Wonsuk Ma and Robert P. Menzies, 337–60. JPTSup 11. Sheffield: Sheffield Academic Press, 1997. The author includes photographs (358–60) taken by Robert P. Menzies (currently a missionary in China) of the Elize's former missionary residence and of the former church building in the "old town" section of Li Jiang, China. Also included here is a photograph of Elize that she has signed "Bidt voor mij" (pray for me).

Land, Steven J. "Pentecostal Spirituality as Apocalyptic Vision; A Narrative-Praxis Analysis." In *Pentecostal Spirituality: A Passion for the Kingdom*, 58–121. JPTSup 1. Sheffield: Sheffield Academic Press, 1993.

Lee, Joyce, and Glenn Gohr. "Women in the Pentecostal Movement." *Enrichment* 4 (Fall, 1999) 60–62. Accessed October 1, 2007. Online: http://enrichmentjournal.ag.org/199904/060_women.cfm.

Luce, Alice E. "From the Mexican Border." *Weekly Evangel* (April 28, 1917) 12. Material cited here by Alice Luce is available from the Flower Pentecostal Heritage Center.

———. "Encouraging Report of the Mexican Work." *Weekly Evangel* (May 19, 1917) 11.

———. "Report of the Mexican Work." *Weekly Evangel* (July 14, 1917) 13.

———. "Open Doors in Mexico." *Weekly Evangel* (November 17, 1917) 13.

———. "Physical Manifestations of the Spirit." *Pentecostal Evangel* (July 27, 1918) 2.

———. "Mexican Work in California." *Christian Evangel* (December 14, 1918) 14.

———. "Paul's Missionary Methods, Parts I, II and III." *Pentecostal Evangel* (January 8, 1921) 6–7; (January 22, 1921) 6, 11; and (February 5, 1921) 6–7.

———. *Pictures of Pentecost*. Springfield, MO: Gospel Publishing House, no date.

———. "The Latin-American Pentecostal Work." *Pentecostal Evangel* (June 25, 1927) 6–7.

———. *The Little Flock in the Last Days*. Springfield, MO: Gospel Publishing House, 1927.

———. "The Great Physician and His Medicine." *Pentecostal Evangel* (September 6, 1930) 6.

———. "Deaf and Dumb Child in Mexico Healed." *Pentecostal Evangel* (February 20, 1932) 11.

———. "What is it to be a Christian?" Tract 34–4661. Springfield, MO: Gospel Publishing House, 1934.

Alice E. Luce, and Henry C. Ball. *Glimpses of Our Latin-American Work in the United States and Mexico*. Springfield, MO: Foreign Missions Department, General Council of the Assemblies of God, 1940.

Lyonnet, Stanislaus. "*Agape* et charismes selon 1 Co 12, 31." In *Paul de Tarse: Apôtre du Notre Temps*, edited by Lorenzo De Lorenzi, 509–27. Série monographique de 'Benedictina' 1. Rome: Abbaye de S. Paul, 1979.

Ma, Julie C. "Elva Vanderbout." In *When the Spirit Meets the Spirits: Pentecostal Ministry among the Kankana-ey Tribe in the Philippines*, 74–86. Studien zur interkulturellen Geschichte des Christentums 118. Frankfurt am Main: Lang, 2000.

MacArthur, John. *1 Corinthians: Godly Solutions for Church Problems*. Nashville, TN: W Publishing Group, 2001.

Macchia, Frank D. "The Kingdom and the Power: Spirit Baptism in Pentecostal and Ecumenical Perspective." In *The Work of the Spirit: Pneumatology and Pentecostalism*, edited by Michael Welker, 109–35. Grand Rapids, MI: Eerdmans, 2006.

Maher, Michael. "A Break with Tradition: Ordaining Women Rabbis," *ITQ* 72 (2007) 32–60.

Marshall, I. Howard. "The First Letter to Timothy: The Theological Story." In *New Testament Theology: Many Witnesses, One Gospel*, 401–405. Downers Grove, IL: InterVarsity, 2004.

Martin, Francis. *Baptism in the Holy Spirit: A Scriptural Foundation*. Steubenville, OH: Franciscan University Press, 1986.

Massey, Presston T. "The Meaning of *katakaluptō* and *kata kephalēs echōn* in I Corinthians 11.2–16." *NTS* 53 (2007) 502–23.

McGee, Gary B. "To the Regions Beyond: The Global Expansion of Pentecostalism." In *The Century of the Holy Spirit: 100 Years of Pentecostal and Charismatic Renewal, 1901–2001*, edited by Vinson Synan, 69–95. Nashville, TN: Nelson, 2001.

McKay, John. "When the Veil is Taken Away: The Impact of Prophetic Experience on Biblical Interpretation." *JPT* 5 (1994) 17–40.

McQueen, Larry R. "The Appropriation of the Themes of Joel in Pentecostalism." In *Joel and the Spirit: The Cry of a Prophetic*

Hermeneutic, 74–106. JPTSup 8. Sheffield: Sheffield Academic Press, 1995.

Menzies, Robert P. "Spirit-Baptism and Spiritual Gifts." In *Pentecostalism in Context: Essays in Honor of William W. Menzies*, edited by Wonsuk Ma and Robert P. Menzies, 48–59. JPTSup 11. Sheffield: Sheffield Academic Press, 1997.

Menzies, William W. "The Methodology of Pentecostal Theology: An Essay on Hermeneutics." In *Essays on Apostolic Themes: Studies in Honor of Howard M. Ervin*, edited by Paul Elbert, 1–14. Eugene, OR: Wipf & Stock, 2007.

Menzies, William W., and Robert P. Menzies. *Spirit and Power, Foundation of Pentecostal Experience: A Call to Evangelical Dialogue*. Grand Rapids, MI: Zondervan, 2000.

Mühlen, Heribert. "Gifts of the Spirit in the congregation, the gift of prophecy, the gift of tongues, socio-critical charisms, the gift of healing." In *A Charismatic Theology: Initiation in the Spirit*, 147–66. Translated by Edward Quinn and Thomas Linton. London: Burns & Oates, 1978.

———. *Kirche wächst von innen: Weg zu einer glaubensgeschichtlich neuen Gestalt der Kirche* (Paderborn: Bonifatius, 1996).

Nance, Lisa. "Exploring the Glass Ceiling: Women Who Minister, A Biblical Perspective." Presented to the Urshan Graduate School of Theology Symposium, 2003. Compact disc of the symposium is available from Urshan Graduate School.

Norris, David S. "Exploring the Glass Ceiling: Women Who Minister, A Contemporary Critique." Presented to the Urshan Graduate School of Theology Symposium, 2003. Compact disc of the symposium is available from Urshan Graduate School.

Ollrog, Wolf-Henning. *Paulus und seine Mitarbeiter: Untersuchungen zu Theorie und Praxis der paulinischen Mission*. WMANT 50. Neukirchen-Vluyn, Neukirchener Verlag, 1979.

———. "*sunergos, sunergeō*," *EDNT* 3.303–304.

Parsons, Mikeal C. "Luke and the *Progymnasmata*: A Preliminary Investigation into the Preliminary Exercises." In *Contextualizing Acts: Lukan Narrative and Greco-Roman Discourse*, edited by Todd Penner and Caroline Vander Stichele, 43–63. SBLSymS 20. Atlanta: Society of Biblical Literature, 2003.

Peterson, Mikeuel. "Led by the Holy Spirit: The Missiological Influence of Alice Eveline Luce." D.Miss. diss., Asbury Theological Seminary, 2007.

Payne, Philip B. "Libertarian Women in Ephesus: Response to D. J. Moo's Article, '1 Timothy 2:11–15, Meaning and Significance.'" *TrinJ* NS2 (1981) 169–97.

Porsche, Felix. *Pneuma und Wort: Ein exegetischer Beitrag zur Pneumatologie des Johannesevangeliums.* FThSt 16. Frankfurt am Main: Knecht, 1974.

de la Potterie, Ignace, and Stanislaus Lyonnet. "Perfection of the Christian 'Led by the Spirit' and Action in the World, According to St. Paul." In *The Christian Lives by the Spirit*, 221–43. Translated by John Morris. Staten Island, NY: Alba House, 1971.

Powers, Janet Everts, "'Your Daughters Shall Prophesy': Pentecostal Hermeneutics and the Empowerment of Women." In *The Globalization of Pentecostalism: A Religion Made to Travel*, edited by Murray W. Dempster et al., 313–37. Irvine, CA: Regnum, 1999.

———. "Pentecostalism 101: Your Daughters Shall Prophesy," In *Philip's Daughters: Women in Pentecostal—Charismatic Leadership*, edited by Amos Yong and Estrelda Alexander. Eugene, OR: Wipf & Stock, forthcoming.

Prosser, Peter E. *Dispensationalist Eschatology and Its Influence on American and British Religious Movements.* Lewiston, NY: Mellen, 1999.

Rea, John. *The Holy Spirit in the Bible: All the Major Passages about the Spirit, A Commentary.* Foreword by J. Rodman Williams. Lake Mary, FL: Creation House, 1990.

Richard, Earl. "Luke: Author and Thinker." In *New Views on Luke and Acts*, 15–32. Collegeville, MN: Liturgical, 1990.

Rios, Elizabeth D. "'The Ladies Are Warriors': Latina Pentecostalism and Faith-Based Activism in New York City." In *Azusa Street & Beyond: 100 Years of Commentary on the Global Pentecostal/ Charismatic Movement*, edited by Grant McClung, 217–29. Gainesville, FL: Bridge-Logos, 2006.

Roebuck, David. "Perfect Liberty to Preach the Gospel: Women Ministers in the Church of God." *Pneuma: Journal of the Society for Pentecostal Studies* 17 (1995) 25–32.

Rooney, Lucy, and Robert Faricy. *Lord, Teach us to Pray: Leader's Manual.* 2nd edition. Vatican City: International Catholic Charismatic Renewal Services, 1998.

Runia, Klass. "Gifts of the Spirit." *RTR* 29 (1970) 82–94.

———. *Op zoek naar de Geest.* Kampen: Kok, 2000.

Russell, E. A. "'They believed Philip Preaching' (Acts 8.12)," *IBS* 1 (1979) 169–76.

Ruthven, Jon. "Charismatic Theology and Biblical Emphases." *EQ* 69 (1997) 217–36.

———. "The 'Foundational Gifts' of Ephesians 2:20." *JPT* 10/2 (2002) 28–43. Accessed October 1, 2007. Online: http://www. logosword.co.uk/articles/eph220_ foundationGifts-1.htm.

Shelton, James B. "Epistemology and Authority in the Acts of the Apostles: An Analysis and Test Case Study of Acts 15:1–29." *The Spirit & Church* 2 (2000) 231–47.

———. *Mighty in Word and Deed: The Role of the Holy Spirit in Luke-Acts*. Eugene, OR: Wipf & Stock, 2000.

———. "'Filled with the Holy Spirit' and 'Full of the Holy Spirit': Lucan Redactional Phrases." In *Faces of Renewal: Studies in Honor of Stanley M. Horton*, edited by Paul Elbert, 80–107. Eugene, OR: Wipf & Stock, 2007.

Smail, Thomas A. "Theology of Renewal and the Renewal of Theology." *Theological Renewal* 1 (1975) 2–4.

Smeeton, Donald Dean. "William Tyndale: A Theologian of Renewal." In *Faces of Renewal: Studies in Honor of Stanley M. Horton*, edited by Paul Elbert, 163–71. Eugene, OR: Wipf & Stock, 2007.

Spencer, Aida Besancon. *Beyond the Curse: Women Called to Minister*. Nashville, TN: Nelson, 1985.

Stanton, Graham N. "Presuppositions in New Testament Criticism." In *New Testament Interpretation: Essays on Principles and Methods*, edited by I. Howard Marshall, 60–71. Exeter: Paternoster, 1977.

Steven, James H. S. *Worship in the Spirit: Charismatic Worship in the Church of England*. Carlisle: Paternoster, 2002.

Stronstad, Roger. *The Charismatic Theology of St. Luke*. Peabody, MA: Hendrickson, 1984.

———. *Spirit, Scripture & Theology: A Pentecostal Perspective*. Baguio City, Philippines: Asia Pacific Theological Seminary, 1995.

———. *The Prophethood of All Believers: A Study of Luke's Charismatic Theology*. JPTSup 16. Sheffield: Sheffield Academic Press, 1999.

Thomas, John Christopher, "Pentecostals, Women and the Bible." *JPT* 5 (1994) 41–56.

———. "Implications for Pentecostal Theology and Ministry." In *The Devil, Disease and Deliverance: Origins of Illness in New Testament Thought*, 310–19. JPTSup 13. Sheffield: Sheffield Academic Press, 1998.

————. "The Spirit in the Fourth Gospel: Narrative Explorations" In *The Spirit of the New Testament*, 157–74. Blandford Forum, Dorset: Deo, 2005.

Trebilco, Paul R. *Jewish Communities in Asia Minor*. New York: Cambridge University Press, 1991.

Williams, Cyril G. *Tongues of the Spirit*. Cardiff: University of Wales Press, 1981.

Williams, J. Rodman. *The Era of the Spirit*. Plainfield, NJ: Logos, 1971.

————. *The Pentecostal Reality*. Plainfield, NJ: Logos, 1972. Accessed October 1, 2007. Online: http:// home.Regent.edu/rodmwil/.

————. "A Reply to The Charismatics: A Doctrinal Perspective." 1979. 17 pages. In *Special Collections*, Regent University Library; Holy Spirit Research Center, Oral Roberts University; and Pentecostal Research Center, Lee University.

————. *The Gift of the Holy Spirit Today*. Plainfield, NJ: Logos, 1980.

————. "Ministry of Women." In *Renewal Theology, III: The Church, The Kingdom, and Last Things,* 210–16. Grand Rapids, MI: Zondervan, 1992.

————. "Biblical Truth and Experience: A Reply to Charismatic Chaos." *Paraclete* 27/3 (1993) 16–30.

Winter, Bruce W. *Roman Wives, Roman Widows: The Appearance of New Women and the Pauline Communities*. Grand Rapids, MI: Eerdmans, 2003.

Wire, Antoinette Clark. *The Corinthian Women Prophets: A Reconstruction Through Paul's Rhetoric*. Minneapolis: Fortress, 1990.

Witt, R. E. *Isis in the Graeco-Roman World: Aspects of Greek and Roman Life*. Ithaca, NY: Cornell University Press, 1971.

Wright, N. T. "The Biblical Basis for Women's Service in the Church." *Priscilla Papers* 20/4 (2006) 5–10.